"Art McNeese explores co ⋯⋯⋯ : will
make us successful when we ⋯⋯⋯ ⋯⋯⋯ ⋯⋯⋯ us to
invert the pyramid by thinking and behaving oppositely to what society
teaches. Doing so will give us strength through weakness—becoming
more Christlike. This book includes twelve lessons that will transform
your life if you choose to practice them. Read *The Power Paradox* today—
it will leave a smile on your soul."

— Scott Seagren, Senior Program Manager, Executive Leadership
Development Experience, Amazon

"Art McNeese's book, *The Power Paradox*, challenges our ideas of what
true strength is. He highlights taking the path of demotion rather than
promotion, bottom-up power, the way up is down, and self-reliance compared to God reliance. This book will promote upside-down thinking
and each of us adopting a Christlike attitude toward living in today's
social media driven world."

— Bill Arnold, Fortune 100 Trainer, author of *Common Sense Success*

"In *The Power Paradox*, Art McNeese has written on a contemporary sub-
ject with clarity and focus. He states his intent and follows the plan. It's
a relatable and engaging perspective that informs and inspires. It will
resonate with readers at a deeper level of spiritual awareness."

— Donald Brake, PhD, Dean Emeritus, Multnomah Biblical Seminary,
and author of *In the Shadow of His Hand*

"*The Power Paradox* expands the 'upside down world' that Jesus offers
those who would follow him. With goofy stories of squirrels caught in toi-
lets to meaningful accounts of Dave Dravecky and others, McNeese uses
real-life situations to turn the reader's heart to the way of Christ. Insight
from his discussion of the Selfie Syndrome will certainly present a more
excellent way for the twenty-first century disciple."

— Larry Henderson, Director, WorldWide Witness, Halbert Center for
Missions and Global Service, Abilene Christian University

"Examining his own and other's stories, McNeese takes us through the conundrum of the Biblical principle 'through weakness they were made strong' (Hebrews 11:34). True strength only comes from God when we submit and seek Him in everything. While James and John, before the cross, both sought glory by asking to sit next to Jesus' throne, we now live in a post-crucifixion and resurrection world where all power comes by giving up ourself, becoming servants, humbly laying instead at Jesus' feet."

—Jeanetta Sanders, retired Research Librarian and follower of Christ

"In *The Power Paradox*, Art McNeese makes a thought-provoking case that true power only comes from relying on Christ wholeheartedly. An immense amount of wisdom, vulnerability, and personal experience is woven throughout this book. It will help anyone hoping to fully experience Christ in their lives to realize the transformative strength that comes from acknowledging our weakness."

—Chris Jorgensen, Founder and Chief Consultant at Convergent Strategy, author of *The Nehemiah Blueprint*

You may never have considered how strength can be a liability and weakness an asset. But in *The Power Paradox*, Art McNeese will convince you with vivid examples and penetrating insights that the only way to live the authentic Christian life is to put your claims to power aside. He shows that only when you yield your meager strength to him can he fill you with his power and use you as an instrument to accomplish his will.

—Thomas Williams, bestselling author and co-author with Josh McDowell of *How to Know God Exists*

"These honest and tender words of a father, as he shares the joys and challenges of lovingly rearing his special needs daughter, will touch your heart. His focus is always on being the hands and feet of Jesus, so Art is a wonderful example to each of us."

—Stephen Allison, PhD., Professor of Psychology & Intercultural Studies, Abilene Christian University

The Power Paradox

***

Winning through Downward Mobility

Art McNeese

This book is dedicated to my four daughters:
Cara, Kim, Haley, and Hannah, who have blessed
my life in more ways than I can express.

Contents

***

Introduction

✳✳✳

WHO DO YOU THINK YOU ARE?

My wife Holly and I were vacationing with other couples in Colorado. We all decided to play a board game together, a game none of us had ever played before. We busted out the game and launched in without taking a careful look at the rules. At one point in the contest, we reached a place where a decision had to be made about what to do next. I immediately jumped in with an assertion about the proper way to play. It's important to point out that I had no more information about the next step than anyone else, and equally important to point out that I came off as a know-it-all. Holly knew she needed to call my hand on my behavior. She quickly blurted out, "Who do you think you are?" We all laughed. I was a bit embarrassed, but she had said exactly what I needed to hear.

Her challenge made me a bit uncomfortable, but it was a healthy reminder that I need to be careful not to be too assertive. To defer to others. Her words prompted me to remember that God summons us to positions of weakness instead of postures of strength.

Instinctively, we tend to exercise clout, assert our power, and showcase our strength. We look for subtle ways to assert ourselves. We don't typically consider weakness an asset. Think about weakness in your own life. If you're like most people, you may run from vulnerability. You may choose self-reliance over God-reliance. You're tempted to follow the cultural philosophy of me-first. You automatically assume that revealing your weaknesses to others is a bad thing. But what if weakness is actually your friend? What if there's more to be gained from a position of weakness than a position of strength?

A few years ago, I purchased the book *Strength Finder* and completed the questionnaire to identify my strengths. There's value in this, but it's telling that I haven't found a bestseller titled *Weakness Finder*. We want to determine and advertise our strengths but we're reticent to even think about our weaknesses. However, God calls us to learn to recognize the value of weakness, the power of emptying ourselves, and opening ourselves up to His strength.

The radically counterintuitive teaching of scripture is that God's power is unleashed in weakness. Since I'll be advocating for weakness throughout this book, let me explain what I mean.

DEFINING WEAKNESS

Maybe it's best to start with a definition of terms. For purposes of this book:

Weakness is not moral atrophy. It is not spiritual compromise. God invites us, even commands us, to be strong in the Lord. But it's those last three words that are operative. Weakness is recognizing our absolute dependence on God. Weakness is acknowledging that apart from Christ, we can do nothing. Weakness is leaning into God with every fiber of our being, realizing that he alone is our Strength. Weakness is affirming our inadequacy and God's adequacy.

Weakness is not cowering in fear. Weakness is not timidity. It is recognizing that God did not give us a spirit of fear but a spirit of power and love and self-control. (2 Timothy 1:7)

Weakness is not assigning a limit to what God can accomplish in us. "Now to Him who by the power at work within us is able to do far more abundantly than all we ask or imagine." (Ephesians 3:21) Weakness is not discounting what God is able to do with the spiritual gifts he has given us. But it is the constant recognition that the exercise of his power requires being hardwired to him.

Weakness is acknowledging our lack of sufficiency and God's complete sufficiency. It affirms that God often does his most powerful work through those who seem the weakest.

God never calls us to a life of moral or spiritual weakness, but he does summon us to a life of dependence on him. We tend to assume that getting ahead is found in exercising muscle instead of exercising meekness.

THE WEAKNESS OF PAUL

The apostle Paul wanted to eliminate weakness from his life. He suffered from what he called a thorn in his flesh. We don't know exactly what it was. But it felt like something sharp and painful stuck in his body. Like being jabbed with a fishing hook deep under your skin. It hurt. A lot. It could have been physical or psychological, or both. Paul pleaded with God to remove the thorn. "Three times I begged the Lord to take it away. Each time he said, 'My grace is all you need. My power works best in weakness.'" (2 Corinthians 12:8–9)

But God decided to say no to Paul's request. Paul explains that God declined "...to keep me from becoming proud." (2 Corinthians 12:7) Paul opens the chapter by talking about the revelations he's received from God. He's oblique about it. He's embarrassed to talk about these revelations because he doesn't want to come off like he's bragging. But he does it in self-defense. His detractors in Corinth are trying to discredit him. They argue that Paul isn't really an apostle. Paul responds, "You need to know that I've had glimpses into paradise. I've seen amazing things, things beyond words."

But God wanted to make sure that Paul didn't get full of himself about these extraordinary visions. He wanted to keep Paul from having a sense of self-importance.

"My power works best in weakness." This sounds contradictory. How can power be exhibited in weakness? But until Paul was weaned from self-sufficiency, God could never maximize the impact of Paul's ministry. God knew that the secret to unleashing his power in Paul was to bring him to a place of absolute dependence. He knew that while Paul may have preferred a posture of strength, his influence would be limited when he tried to operate under his own power.

In a competitive culture, the temptation is to look for ways to one-up other people. It's all about that little suffix—ER. We want to demonstrate that we're pretti-er, handsome-er, smart-er, fast-er, wealthi-er than other people. We don't actually take pride in having something but in having more of it than someone else. It's not enough to be thin. We have to be skinnier than she is. It's not enough to be ripped. We must be more buff than he is. We think success is being bigger, better, or badder than someone else. For some people, this results in a 'compare and despair' attitude. One therapist calls this 'comparisonitis.' It's an emotional sickness that can do severe damage to our souls.

But some don't feel any need to win through performance or playing the game of comparison. They exhibit the power of weakness without even realizing their powerlessness. They are content with who they are. Some people live with such disabilities that they are unable to perform even the simplest tasks. The irony is that some of the most powerful lessons in life are learned from the least powerful.

We're all familiar with oxymorons, figures of speech with one or two words in which seemingly contradictory terms appear side by side. Jumbo shrimp. Crash landing. Definite maybe. Friendly takeover. Loyal opposition. Minor miracle. Negative growth.

This book proposes another seeming contradiction. Power through weakness. At first glance, these words don't fit together. In fact, in the eyes of our culture, they are poles apart. The conventional wisdom in our society is that power is always achieved through force, never through surrender. Power is a function of brute strength, not through conceding our position. The unspoken understanding is that leaders eat first, not last. Only an idiot would choose a posture of weakness if he is trying to get ahead.

But the reality is that enduring power exudes from weakness. Not weakness in the sense of being flimsy or gullible or being a pushover. Not weakness that capitulates when moral firmness is demanded. But weakness that recognizes one's need for strength from God. Weakness that grows out of the acknowledgment of his adequacy and our inadequacy. The Power Paradox is that genuine strength doesn't come from strong arming our way, but from surrender. Real strength doesn't mean always having the upper hand—it means being willing to take the lower place in life.

I invite you to discover the immense strength that emerges from humility.

CHAPTER 1

The Power of Peggy

***

God had looked for a man weak enough, and He found me.
—Hudson Taylor, founder of the China Inland
Mission, on the secret of his success

OUR DAUGHTER, HANNAH

OUR DAUGHTER, HANNAH, WAS BORN with a severe birth defect. Hannah is twenty-seven years old, but she has the intellect of a two-year-old. Hannah has never spoken a word. We call her our little 'wordless one.' But God has faithfully taken care of Hannah and used her in countless ways.

One of the greatest blessings in our lives was Hannah's year in first grade. Peggy Taylor was Hannah's first-grade teacher. Peggy is a believer in Christ and a close friend. We knew she would be a wonderful teacher, but we had no idea what Peggy's teaching would mean in the lives of all those first graders.

Here's how Peggy described what happened.

I believe God had a plan for Hannah and me. I had started to pray and plan how Hannah could be successful in first grade. On the first day of school, when Hannah wasn't in the room yet, I had the kids alone for the first time. I prayed that the right words would come as I explained to the children for the first time what an EXTRA special class this was because they were chosen to be in this room! They were selected to be here because of one 'super special' thing that each one of them had. They were sitting in this room because they had 'A Heart for Hannah.' As I looked at this group of children, their eyes twinkled, and big smiles came across their faces!

At that point, we talked about Hannah and what we knew about her and what we remembered from kindergarten—a few had been in her class the year before and had some firsthand experience. We discussed how she is like us in some ways and different from us in some ways—that just because she doesn't talk to us doesn't necessarily mean she doesn't understand us. How we need to talk to her just like we would any other friend. There were several questions—many I could answer, some I could not. But here was a captive audience, ready to greet their new friend!

They welcomed Hannah that day with a love and compassion that grew as the year went on. The innocence of these children and the simple faith that they have in life was so refreshing! It was a daily reminder to never give up!

Through the growth of our year, the learning was daily. We took many teachable moments to set Hannah up for success. Soon, the children began to initiate help with Hannah on their own. The children were such encouragers—I began to see this in the way they started treating each other too! They helped Hannah when she tried to walk in line. They would fuss as to who would get to sit next to her at lunch. They would play with her at recess, they would push her on the swings, walk with her on the playground, help her through calendar time, and every day, they took turns reading stories to her.

When Hannah would start laughing, the kids would look in her eyes and say, "Tell me what is so funny!" By taking care of the WEAK, these little seeds were growing into such beautiful strong flowers! There were many teachable opportunities where I stopped and reminded the kids of the things we do automatically—that we take for granted, that Hannah has to work VERY hard to accomplish.

One particular day in January, I told Hannah to go get her lunch and come get in line—I asked the kids not to say anything to her that day so we could see if she could do this on her own with me just telling her once. As everyone gathered in line with lunches, we were quietly watching Hannah as she walked to her cubby. She slowly opened the door, took out her lunch, closed the door, and walked to the line! As she got herself in line the class erupted with cheers. "Did ya see that??!! WOW! She did it!" The class began to cheer and shout, and I did, too! I will never forget the excitement of that moment. We celebrated what seemed like such a small thing, but they knew it was a great accomplishment for Hannah. I celebrated the class's understanding of that moment.

"We had many days of wonderful celebrations with Hannah. I watched the children get excited when she unzipped her lunch box or finished a puzzle or pushed in her chair when asked to come to the carpet or when she correctly pointed to an object in a book. As the school year closed, this class had grown into a wonderful bouquet of flowers. As our year came to an end, we reminisced about our time together and all we had done in first grade.

"We talked about what good friends we all had become and what wonderful friends they had been to Hannah. **I shared with the class that my wish for them was that they would always have a 'Heart for Hannah.'** That they would always be there to help those, like Hannah, who were not as strong as themselves and that their heart would always reach out to be an encourager to others, just like they had been with Hannah.

At the end of the year, Peggy took pictures of Hannah with each of her classmates. She also asked each student to write entries in their journal about Hannah. Then she put those little notes together in a scrapbook and gave it to Holly and me. What a treasure! Peggy had used the year to teach those children to serve the weak, and the whole class had learned invaluable lessons in giving and serving.

I could write volumes about the lessons found in what the kids wrote. It's amazing what we can learn from children. But I witnessed firsthand the power of weakness. We tend to nudge weak people into the background. We avoid the poor. We honor kids with high IQs and cheer for the best athletes on Friday nights. We don't usually recognize people who struggle. We typically don't stop to honor those who care for the weak. But I want you to see that this is the exact opposite of God's value system.

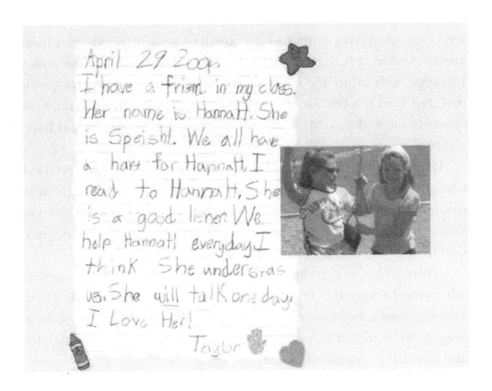

April 29 200_
I have a friend in my class.
Her name is Hannah. She
is Speishl. We all have
a hart for Hannah. I
read to Hannah. She
is a good listener. We
help Hannah everyday. I
think She understras
us. She will talk one day.
I Love Her!
Taybr

Hannah is one of the weakest people I know. But God has used Hannah to teach others unforgettable lessons. Weak people are often exceptional tutors.

Some think of special needs people as a burden when the reality is, they are a blessing. It is Hannah's very weakness that makes her a singular gift to our family. Hannah can't say, "I love you," but we feel and experience her affection in waves. She doesn't have the ability or need to compare herself to anyone else. She can't brag about any awards. For Hannah, God's love is more important than the praise of others. Hannah can't really 'do' anything (other than feed herself with some help), but she accomplishes much.

Hannah is vulnerable but powerful. The reality is, I am just as weak and vulnerable as she is. In fact, given her vulnerability, I wonder who is handicapped and who isn't. Maybe my disability is greater than hers.

When people brought their children to Jesus, the disciples wanted to send them away. Why bother with a bunch of weak little kids? But Jesus knew the value of being with children, with the weak. One of the things I struggle with in my life is self-sufficiency. Maybe you can relate with that. But God teaches me through Hannah. When I'm with her, God speaks to me and says, "The only things that matter are faith and hope and love."

Hannah teaches me to trust. Hannah teaches me to love. So, God taps me on the shoulder every day and says, "Art, I want you to learn to trust, to learn to love." I sincerely believe if the only thing I was given to do for the rest of my life is to take care of Hannah, I could do it, because God has planted love for Hannah deep in my heart.

Hannah lives in a group home in Texas. She shares the house with other women who are physically and intellectually challenged. There are numerous lessons to be learned from these women. None of these women are competitive with the others—there's a spirit of deference and love that pervades the house.

Maybe the key is that none of these women are self-conscious. They feel no need to groom their images because they have no desire to one-up anyone else. They have no need to look good in front of others— many have to be bathed and dressed by others. Image doesn't matter to these women as they have no image to protect or embellish. These women are, for the most part, emptied of themselves. They have eluded the siren call of self-promotion.

THE POWER OF THE POWERLESS

Christopher de Vinck tells about what he learned from his special needs brother Oliver. Oliver lay in the same bed for thirty-three years. He couldn't see, walk, communicate, or feed himself. But he touched the lives of hundreds of people. He taught them the meaning of courage and perseverance. The following excerpt is from the deeply moving story of Oliver written by his brother, Christopher de Vinck, who discovered through Oliver's life, the power of the powerless.

For thirty-three years Oliver lived in an upstairs bedroom, a child of light, a true innocent who never caused any trouble, never broke a commandment, never wronged another human being. Mother was confined to the house, alone and without the support of relatives or friends... This enforced seclusion was difficult for me; I had a restless, seeking spirit. Through a solitude where I could 'prepare the way of the Lord.' Sorrow opened my heart, and I 'died.' I underwent this 'death' unaware that it was a trial by fire from which I would rise renewed—more powerfully, more consciously alive..."

Oliver's weakness resulted in Christopher's death to self and a new life in which he was 'more consciously alive.'[1]

Henri Nouwen left his teaching post at Harvard to go to Daybreak, a community of mentally and physically handicapped people. He cared for Adam, a twenty-five-year-old man who couldn't speak, dress himself, and who suffered from severe seizures. Nouwen talked about what he learned from serving Adam. "Adam was the weakest person in our community, but the most powerful. Adam creates a quiet rhythm in the house. Adam prompts words of affection and gentleness."[2]

Someone questioned Nouwen about whether this was really the best use of his time, a Harvard professor spending his days brushing teeth and taking Adam to the bathroom. Nouwen said, "I'm not giving up anything. It is I, not Adam, who gets the main benefit from our friendship." Most people would have written off Adam as pathetically weak. But Adam represents the power of the powerless.

STRENGTH DISGUISED AS WEAKNESS

David Ransom was a member of our church. He was severely disabled and blind from birth. His brain had been accidentally oxygen-deprived, and the consequences were severe. In adulthood, David developed heart trouble and diabetes. Near the end of his life, both of his legs were amputated below the knee.

But David was a tower of strength. With a keen mind, he memorized most of the tax code and worked for the IRS, providing information to people calling in with tough questions about their returns. David also memorized much of the Bible and could recite many passages word for word. He taught my older daughter's sixth-grade Bible class. At the opening session of the class, he had students go around the room and give their names. He then had each student's name memorized instantly. He would call on the appropriate student to read Bible passages or answer questions. He left an indelible impact on those students.

Most people would say David was weak. But David knew that God was his strength. So David taught us and served us. He knew that God's power is made perfect in weakness.

WHAT DOES IT MEAN TO BE WEAK?

Weakness means praying for God's hand to be with us. Weakness is asking God to do something in us that we could never do ourselves. Weakness means humbling ourselves and connecting with the cross of Christ every day. Weakness means recognizing our dependence on God each and every moment. It means starting every day with the prayer, "God, take our weakness and exchange it for Strength."

It means affirming that you're powerless as a parent to raise your kids unless you have the strength of God. It means acknowledging that you don't have any control over much of what happens to you but that God has complete control. It means placing your ministry in the hands of God and asking him to bless it because you're empty of any power to bless it. It means you embrace humility in your marriage and ask God to make you a better husband or a better wife.

I believe God is leading me through a life-long training program in discovering the power of weakness. This is not training that I always welcome. I have sometimes been like Jacob, wrestling with God and resisting God's coaching. It's easy for us to stubbornly choose to grapple with God, trying to flex our muscles instead of yielding to his strength.

What do you want for your life? If you're looking to unleash infinite power, you must first learn the unlimited strength that emerges from weakness. In the next few chapters, I invite you to join me on a journey as we explore in detail 'the power of downward mobility.'

PRAYER:

"Father, I recognize that I have no power of my own. I affirm that I have no sufficiency in myself. Without you, I can't do anything. But now I want to claim the power that comes from your offer of Strength. I want to trade in my weakness in exchange for your power. I ask you to replace my brokenness with your wholeness. I ask you to take my inability and replace it with your ability. I ask you to help me realize that when I am weak, then I am strong. Thank you for the promise of unlimited strength. Thank you for promising not only to give me strength but to give me Yourself. Because you are the greatest Strength of all. Always remind me that your power is made perfect in weakness. In the name of the one who was crucified in weakness but raised in Strength, Amen."

PRACTICAL SUGGESTION:

Let me give you a little assignment. Pick out someone you consider to be weak. It could be someone who's disabled or poor or challenged in some significant way. Then make a commitment to serve that person or those people this month. It could involve serving meals or providing transportation or being a friend to somebody who's usually left out. If you're a teacher, choose a child in your class who needs encouragement. If you're a teenager, choose somebody at school nobody else pays attention to. If you're a parent, take your child to visit someone who's hurting. Pray for God to show you the weak people around you who need your love. Then write down a few lines about what you learned in the process. I guarantee, God will use that experience to bless your life.

DISCUSSION QUESTIONS:

1. Have you ever had a significant experience with someone who is special needs? What was that like? Do you believe that you learned anything from that experience?
2. Read 1 Corinthians 1:25–27. How does God use the foolish to shame the wise?
3. Read 1 Thessalonians 5:14. What are some of the ways you can take care of those who are weak?
4. How do you believe God often uses those who are weak to teach us?

CHAPTER 2

The Power of Downward Mobility

***

May all your expectations be frustrated, may all your plans be thwarted, may all your desires be withered into nothingness, that you may experience the powerlessness and poverty of a child and sing and dance in the love of God who is Father, Son, and Spirit.

—Larry Hein

A BICYCLE RACE IN INDIA defies expectations. The object of the race is to go the shortest distance possible within a specified time. At the start of the race, everybody queues up at the line. When the gun sounds, all the bicycles, as best they can, stay put. Racers are disqualified if they tip over or one of their feet touches the ground. So they inch forward just enough to keep the bike balanced. When the time is up and another gun sounds, the person who has gone the farthest is the loser, and the person closest to the starting line is the winner.

Jesus gives us the rules to the eternal race of life. The finish line is painted on the other side of our deaths. Right in front of the throne of God himself. The winning strategy is caring about others and not about ourselves. It is letting others go first. Not pushing to the front. It is being humble, as Jesus was humble.

But this is counter to the way we normally think. We're prone to automatically race ahead of others and push ourselves to the front of the line. This has a devastating impact on our view of ourselves. We're often convinced that our values and identity are the result of how we stack up against others. We are vulnerable to the tendency to define ourselves in terms of the image we project, rather than the image of God within us. To have a healthy sense of our identity, we need to recapture the original design for self. And where better to do this than by looking at the One who was the perfect image of God?

Christ could have fallen victim to the temptation to compete and compare. To the desire to advance himself. But in Philippians 2, Paul says that even though Christ was in very nature God, he did not consider equality with God something to be grasped. Jesus was co-equal with God the Father. Jesus was not an assistant to God. He has never been a junior partner to God. He is equal with the Father in every way, shape, and form.

But instead of promoting himself, he surrendered himself. Pause for a moment and think about what it was like to leave divinity for humanity. Angels had hovered around Jesus with anthems of praise. But now, he accepts the limitations of being human. He is born in the armpit of the world. He gets sick like we do and suffers like we do. He knows what it is to be lonely and tired and filled with horror and dread. People have tried to illustrate this transition. It would be like a man condescending to the position of an ant, crawling around like an ant. But the analogy breaks down. It's one thing for a creature to condescend to a lower rank of creation. It's something else for the Creator to become a creature. There's an enormous chasm between the transcendent God and human beings like you and me. We can't really imagine how violent and profane the transition was for Christ.

> Philip Yancey writes, "People expect power from their God, not powerlessness, strength not weakness, largeness not smallness."

Consider that Jesus has eternally been a servant. He didn't become a servant in the incarnation. The preexistent Christ had been a servant for all of eternity. The Father, Son, and Holy Spirit have eternally deferred to each other and honored each other. Jesus wasn't slumming it when he served. He was just acting out of the depth of his character. The member of the Godhead we know as Jesus demonstrated for thirty-three years what he had been for all of eternity. Christ had the option of coming with a splash of publicity, but instead, he came in obscurity. Our model is the unassuming servant who never coveted recognition. Paul said, "He made himself nothing."

Christ could have been born into royalty like King Charles. He had the option of being born into money like a Rockefeller. He could have chosen the spotlight of celebrity. Instead, he chose a life of poverty, obscurity, and weakness. Rather than chasing after upward mobility, he consistently moved down the ladder.

Sadly, we move in the opposite direction. We humans seem irresistibly drawn to climbing upward and to self-promotion. Where did all of this originate? Narcissism was born in the Garden of Eden when Adam and Eve shook their puny fists at God. It commenced the moment they chose to elevate themselves above God.

Inherently, we turn in on ourselves because we all have Adam's spiritual DNA. We're corrupted by a sin nature. We're possessed with a self-focus instead of a God-focus. That's why we want to exalt self. Promote self.

> Years ago, my wife and I visited Cancun for a vacation. We checked into one of those all-inclusive resorts. At the registration desk, I asked if we might have a room with some additional privacy. I was expecting the usual, "Sorry, sir, but all our rooms are full." Instead, the clerk at the desk said, "How about the presidential suite?" I responded, "At no additional cost?" He said, "Yes." I jumped at the chance. "Yes, thanks so much." I walked out to the lobby ready to haul our bags up to the luxurious room. A bellman pulled up with a golf cart and said, "You El Presidente?" To which I responded, "I am today." We were then ushered up to an elaborate room. I have reflected on that moment when he asked, "You El Presidente?" There's something in most of us that wants to be president, that wants to sit at the top. But maybe we need to change the trajectory.

PROMOTING GOD

Instead of promoting ourselves, we need to promote God. Jesus always put the Father ahead of himself, above himself. Here's the irony: Jesus' descent resulted in a stunning paradox. Descending actually meant moving up. "Therefore God exalted him to the highest place and gave him the name that is above every name." (Philippians 2:9) Jesus spiraled downward into death itself. But death couldn't hold him. Because God raised him from the dead three days later and elevated him to the highest place. Since Jesus died to self, he was exalted.

How do we learn to emulate Christ in dying to ourselves?

It all begins with embracing our value in Christ.

A POP QUIZ

Let me give you a quick pop quiz. Which of these statements is true?

    a.   God loves us because Jesus died for us.
    b.   Jesus died for us because God loves us.

The first statement actually sounds pretty spiritual. Jesus saw our need, so he died for us. And that means now God is free to love us. We've received the righteousness of Christ, so now God can love us and put up with us. But that isn't true. God doesn't love us just because Jesus died for us. Jesus died for us because God loved us. He loved us first. Before we did anything and before Jesus did anything. God loved us before Jesus ever went to the cross. He loved us when we couldn't have cared less for Him. God's forgiveness is not a grudging acceptance of us just because of what Jesus did.

If you're a Christian, remember: You'll never be more forgiven than you are right now. You'll never be more loved than you are right now. You've already arrived, and you're already accepted. That doesn't mean God is finished changing you. He will keep working on you until the day you die. He will use his Holy Spirit to transform you and change you. But God's love for you won't be any greater for you tomorrow than it is today.

Once we experience Christ's love, we learn to die to self.

BAPTISM IS A BURIAL

This death is experienced and affirmed in baptism. Do you understand the significance of baptism? Paul teaches that baptism is dying to yourself. Just as Jesus died, was buried, and then raised, we die to sin and self, are buried, and then raised. We say goodbye to self and hello to Christ. In baptism, the old self died. And a new self came into being. You received a new identity in Christ. Qualification in Christ frees you to die to self and live for others.

Paul uses the first five chapters of Romans to teach the great doctrine of salvation by grace. But he knew that Roman Christians were tempted to presume on grace. So Paul reminds them that baptism was the moment in which they died to sin. "Well then, should we keep on sinning so that God can show us more and more of his wonderful grace? Of course not. Since we have died to sin, how can we continue to live in it? Or have you forgotten that when we were joined with Christ Jesus in baptism, we joined him in his death?" (Romans 6:1–3)

In the early church, people were often baptized in a church-adjacent building called a baptistery, shaped like a Roman funeral building. Early Christians built these baptismal houses to remind their converts: *Baptism means your death to self! You are going through a spiritual union with Christ. He is actually with you in this moment. You share in his death, burial, and resurrection. The old sinful nature dies and the new you, led by the Spirit, comes to life.* Paul put it this way: "I have been crucified with Christ, it is no longer I who live, but Christ who lives in me." (Galatians 2:20) "No longer I who live…" It's not even me.

Paul writes, "But thanks be to God, who always leads us in triumphal procession in Christ…" (2 Corinthians 2:14) Think about the movie *Gladiator* with Russell Crowe where Roman generals dragged prisoners of war back into Rome. Imagine those prisoners being paraded through the streets of Rome as a sign of Rome's victory. That's the scene Paul is giving us. Roman armies marched the prisoners of war through the streets.

The prisoners were bound in chains. Defeated captives. And if you were one of those prisoners, you knew you'd been conquered. Paul says we're not the ones leading the procession. We're the prisoners being led by God. We belong to God. He's in charge—we're not. We belong to him, so there's no need to weigh ourselves down with constant comparisons.

People who have died to themselves resist the pressure to compare. People who have been conquered for Christ understand the power of weakness.

Through the years, I have interviewed many candidates for employment with two questions. First, I ask, "What are your greatest strengths?" Second, I ask, "What is your greatest weakness?" The second question often puts the candidate in an awkward position. On the one hand, if she can't identify a weakness, she risks coming off as arrogant. On the other hand, if she confesses to a weakness, she might not get hired.

I read about a manager being interviewed for a new position. "My department has turned a profit every quarter for the past five years," the candidate says. "I've never had a personnel problem, and I've always gotten superior performance reviews." "Very impressive," the interviewer replied. "And what's your greatest weakness?" "I tend to exaggerate."

To tap into the power of weakness, we must come clean about the Achilles' heels in our lives. God isn't calling us to parade our faults or advertise our weaknesses, but he is summoning us to acknowledge them and rely on him for strength. He is inviting us to say no to the relentless temptation to compare and compete.

The challenge is to choose to move down the ladder instead of scratching our way to the top. "Don't compare yourself with others. Each of you must take responsibility for doing the creative best you can with your own life" (Galatians 6:4–5) It is embarrassing to realize that while we are scrambling to the top of the ladder, we meet Christ, who is on his way down.

PRAYER:

"Father, teach me that you call me to a life of downward mobility. Give me the presence of your Holy Spirit to beckon me to follow in the downward steps of Jesus. Help me to be impervious to the voices that constantly tug me in the direction of success and power. Enable me to embrace the cross as the principle of my life. Remind me that the way up is down. In the name of the One before whom every knee will someday bow."

PRACTICAL SUGGESTION:

Find a way in which you can serve so that nobody knows. Be part of the 'secret service.'

DISCUSSION QUESTIONS:

1. What are some of the pressures you experience to keep moving up instead of down in our culture?
2. What impact do you think advertising has on our tendency to move up?
3. Read Romans 6:1–4. What is the meaning of baptism?
4. Read Philippians 2:1–10. Revisit the steps that Jesus took to move down the ladder. Read Philippians 2:19–30. How did Timothy and Epaphroditus personify the spirit of Christ?
5. What is the most significant barrier in your life against downward mobility?

CHAPTER 3

Power from the Bottom-Up

✳✳✳

At the age of six I wanted to be a cook. At seven I wanted to be Napoleon. And my ambition has been growing ever since.

—Salvador Dali

THREE RICE UNIVERSITY STUDENTS FROM Martel College drew inspiration from comic book character Spider-Man and put their creative and engineering skills to work building a replica of Peter Parker's bedroom for Willy Week, when each residential college participates in themed activities. While the other colleges typically build floats for a parade, Martel often goes one step further by constructing interactive sets they call 'builds.' Sophomore Jonathan Bunt, junior Gigi Rill, and freshman Amanda Suarez spent about two months designing and constructing the room.[3]

With the goal of making the space as authentic as possible, they decorated the room with blinds, a desk strewn with some of Rill's old homework, headphones, and a shelf outfitted with graduated cylinders.

Do you realize that Jesus turned the world upside down? Jesus introduced a world where everything was turned on its head. Where everything was inverted.

It was a brand-new kingdom. Now when we think of the word kingdom, we usually think of something geographical. A chunk of land over which a king rules. But when Jesus used the word kingdom, he wasn't talking about a piece of real estate. He was talking about the rule and the reign of God in people's lives. And the kingdom of God is an upside-down kingdom.

Imagine a kingdom where:

Everything on the top is on the bottom. Everything on the bottom is on the top.
The first are last, and the last are first.
The strong are weak, and the weak are strong.
The rich are poor, and the poor are rich.
Imagine a kingdom where everything is upside down.

Imagine a world where we find by losing. We receive by giving. We're elevated by being humble. We rule by serving. We live by dying. Imagine living in an upside-down world. Where nothing is quite like you expect it to be. Where all the conventional wisdom is challenged.

The kingdom of God is a world of surprises. Where things are different than they appear to be. That's the kind of kingdom Jesus introduced.

"An argument started among the disciples as to which of them would be the greatest. Jesus, knowing their thoughts, took a little child and had him stand beside him. Then he said to them, 'Whoever welcomes this little child in my name welcomes me; and whoever welcomes me welcomes the one who sent me. For he who is least among you all—he is the greatest.'" (Luke 9: 46–48)

Now the shocking thing about this text is that Jesus has just announced that He's on His way to a cross. "Listen carefully to what I am about to tell you: The Son of Man is going to be betrayed into the hands of men." (Luke 9:44) Luke goes on to say they didn't understand what it meant. It's not so much that they misunderstood betrayal. It's that they couldn't make any sense out of this. They thought Jesus was the long-awaited King. That Jesus would set up a political kingdom and beat the Romans into the ground. That Jesus would be a king with clout. So how could Jesus suffer at the hands of other people? It was the opposite of what they'd expected.

But the disciples launch into a debate about which one will be the greatest. Jesus has just announced that he's on his way to death, and they argue about their rankings. Who will be the top dog? Jesus has a little child stand beside him. Now children in the ancient world were barely seen and not heard at all. Judaism gave more respect to kids than other cultures. But even in Judaism, it was often considered a waste of time to teach a child under twelve the Jewish law. So, kids were considered unimportant, even dispensable.

But Jesus never writes off the children. He says, "Whoever welcomes this little child in my name welcomes me; and whoever welcomes me welcomes the one who sent me." (Mark 9:37) To receive a child is to receive Christ, and to receive Christ is to receive the Father. Jesus is saying that even the lowest person on the ladder is significant.

We live in a culture where status is everything. We're all about rankings. We rank football teams and fantasy football teams. We list the Fortune 500. But it's much more personal than that, right? We want to be considered people of status. We want people to think we're smarter or richer or more beautiful. We want to drive fancier cars and live in finer houses and show off more expensive clothes. Our culture says the path to greatness is climbing to the top, getting ahead, working to be in first place, being the boss. In other words, greatness is being king of the hill.

But Jesus mounts a furious challenge against all that. Jesus says it's just the reverse. Jesus establishes a new world order. Where the kingdom and the culture are on a collision course. Jesus says greatness isn't being at the top of the ladder—it's being at the bottom of the ladder. You don't find greatness in scrambling to the front of the line—you find greatness in going to the back of the line.

The famous American doctor Albert Schweitzer was returning from Africa on furlough. He was arriving by train, and the reporters were there to meet him. They waited for him in the first-class section, but he didn't appear. They looked down the line and saw him getting out of the third-class section. They asked, "Why does a world celebrity like you travel in third class?" He responded, "Because there is no fourth class." Jesus tells us to take the lowest places. That's what greatness is about. Striving for status creates a spirit of elitism. It's like a cancer. It creates cliques and a feeling of superiority.

It's fascinating: Jesus defines greatness without making comparisons. We usually measure greatness by comparing ourselves to someone else. But Jesus says that greatness is an attitude; it's a spirit of humility, and it doesn't require someone else's lack of greatness.

Jesus is not opposed to greatness, but he clears away the fog about what greatness really is. Sometimes, we think Jesus is opposed to ambition. We think God frowns on people who want to be great. But that isn't true. God wants us to achieve. He wants us to aspire to great things. He wants us to want greatness. But he wants us to understand that greatness is never found in climbing to the top—it's always found in scooting to the bottom.

IN GOD'S KINGDOM, EVERYBODY CAN BE GREAT

The cool thing about greatness in the kingdom of God is that everybody can be great.

In the world's view of greatness, only a privileged few can be great. It's a pyramid, right? All the nobodies are at the bottom of the pyramid. There's only room for a few at the top. But Jesus takes the pyramid, and he turns it upside down. He inverts the pyramid. And there's room for everybody at the top. There's no limit to the number of people who can be great. Anybody who chooses to serve can achieve greatness. So, Jesus is not opposed to greatness; he wants you to pursue greatness.

Jesus is not just calling us to an illusion; he is calling us to the ultimate reality. Let's be honest: It's easy to think all this talk about greatness through service is just a bunch of garbage. A bunch of words. It's like the *Far Side* cartoon that pictures a dog listening to people as they talk to each other. What the people hear are words. But what the dog hears is this: "Blah-blah, blah-blah, blah-blah, blah-blah." It doesn't mean anything.

Our reaction to an upside-down kingdom may be: "Get serious. It's nice to talk about greatness through service. But we all know that service is for losers. The movers and shakers in the world are the achievers." Sometimes, we look at people who serve others and we think of them as poster children for a way of life we admire but a way of life we would never seriously consider. We give a nod to Mother Teresa, but we still think Bill Gates is the model of success.

Think about it. The American way of life is about winning. Achieving high scores on your SAT. Getting the corner office. Winning the game. Vince Lombardi was a legendary coach who led the Packers to three Super Bowl wins. He said, "Winning's not everything. It's the only thing." That pretty much sums up our philosophy. We think serving other people is a commendable thing to do. But we think the real winners are the people who have proved they belong at the top. But that isn't reality. The reality is that being on top in the world means you're potentially at the bottom.

DON'T TAKE THE BEST SEATS

You see this in Luke 14. Jesus says, when somebody invites you to a big banquet, don't take the best seats. Because somebody more distinguished than you may have been invited. If that happens, you're going to be embarrassed when the host comes and says, "Move over, I reserved that seat for somebody else." You're better off grabbing the cheap seats. Then maybe the host will come and say, "Friend, move up to a better place." "For everyone who exalts himself will be humbled. And he who humbles himself will be exalted." (Luke 14:11)

Jesus makes me start twisting in my seat. A seat I should never have grabbed for myself in the first place. A seat that I may have to give up because I was so presumptuous. We think the way to greatness is to assert ourselves. To strut our stuff. To step up and take the places of honor at the banquet. But Jesus says the way to greatness is to be humble.

Then there's the classic story of reversal in Luke 16. There's a rich man who wears expensive suits and handcrafted shoes and eats gourmet meals every day. Below his table is Lazarus. Lazarus begs for scraps. He's covered with sores. The dogs come and lick his sores. The two men die. The rich man goes to torment. Lazarus goes to paradise.

Everything is turned upside down. And now, the rich man is the beggar. He begs for relief from his pain. "Please have pity on me and send Lazarus to dip the tip of his finger in water and cool my tongue because I am in agony in this fire." But in Jesus' story, there's no turning back. The rich man lived it up on Earth while Lazarus was in pain. And now, they have to trade places. Everything is reversed.

The call to be a servant is not some exceptional call reserved for rare people who have a noble spirit: it's a call for every follower of Christ. When God makes a list of great people, he doesn't list the high achievers of the world and then attach a little p.s. at the bottom, listing the people who served. He makes a list of people who served, and nobody else makes the list. If you achieve something in this world but you don't serve, your name doesn't make the list. Because achievement has nothing to do with greatness.

If you really want to be great, you need to be intentional about moving to the bottom of the ladder. This is a huge challenge. Because it is so counterintuitive. This takes at least three shifts.

First, you have to ask for a new way of thinking. Everything in our culture drives us to reach for the top. We don't think like Jesus thinks. We automatically assume that success means more money and more authority and more acclaim. So, we have to ask God for a new mindset. We must ask for a new way of looking at the world. We have to realize that we've been looking at the world upside down. We need a new reality. The new reality is just the opposite of the old reality. The new reality is that success means serving. Greatness means giving. Honor means humbling yourself.

Now, you can't get there by yourself. This takes God at work. Jesus said, "...how much more will the Father in Heaven give the Holy Spirit to those who ask Him?" (Luke 11:13) The Holy Spirit can retool our minds and hearts. The Holy Spirit can revolutionize our thinking. Most of us live in default mode. We automatically think the world has it right. That success means a bigger house and a Rolex watch and taking home the soccer trophy. So, we have to ask God for brand-new brains. Brains that automatically think of success in terms of less. Tom Sine wrote a book with this title: *Why Settle for More and Miss the Best?* We have to ask God for a new way of thinking.

> God... is not in the business of helping the humanly strong become stronger; rather he takes the weak and makes them strong in Himself. —Erwin Lutzer

Here's the second shift: You have to take bold and decisive action. Someone said, "It's easier to act your way into a new way of thinking than it is to feel your way into a new way of acting." Someone else put it this way, "I hear and I forget. I see and I remember. I do and I understand. For this has become my own." It's like Nike says, "Just do it." When Jesus called the disciples, He didn't say think about whether you want to follow me and then make a decision. He said, "Come and follow me." Right now. Leave your fishing nets. Walk away from doing your own thing to follow me.

C.S. Lewis writes: "The terrible thing, the almost impossible thing, is to hand over your whole self—all your wishes and precautions—to Christ. But it is far easier than what we are all trying to do instead. For what we are trying to do is to remain what we call 'ourselves,' to keep personal happiness as our great aim in life, and yet at the same time to be 'good'…If I want to produce wheat, the change must go deeper than the surface. It must be ploughed up and re-sown."[4]

For most of us, this kind of radical change will never happen unless we make some deliberate decisions about how we live. That means we choose to live counterculturally. We choose downward mobility instead of upward mobility. We choose less instead of more. We choose to serve instead of being served. Maybe it means refusing the promotion. Maybe it means choosing a career that's more about serving than success. Maybe it means walking away from the spotlight.

Whatever it is, ask God to show you what you need to do and then do it. It's time for us to take the challenge of Jesus seriously. It's time for us to live by kingdom values.

Here's the third shift: Stay relentlessly connected to the body of Christ. Other Christians help us see the areas where we need to be broken. "Faithful are the wounds of a friend" (Proverbs 27:6)—whether that friend is a pastor, a parent, a partner, or another believer who loves us enough to point out our spiritual growth areas. Live with the roof off and the walls down.

Other people sometimes serve as a counter to our pride. One of my favorite stories is the legendary exchange between Winston Churchill and Lady Astor. Lady Astor: "Sir Winston, if you were my husband, I would poison your coffee." Churchill: "If you were my wife, I would drink it." Sir Winston had quickly put her in her place.

I was sitting in a hot tub at Pepperdine University, overlooking the shores of Malibu Beach. Sadly, my companions in the jacuzzi were a bunch of my minister buddies. I was wishing that my wife, Holly, could miraculously appear and take their place.

We were having a casual conversation when I mentioned a ministry couple that we all knew. I had met the husband many times but had never met his wife. Now I need to explain at this point that the husband, while a brilliant writer and lecturer, was nothing special to look at. A kind and wonderful man, for sure, but he was not going to be confused with Brad Pitt. Earlier that day, I had met his wife, who was strikingly beautiful. This left me a bit confused as I would never have paired up the two.

That's when I committed a major gaffe. I opened my big mouth and said something like this to my buddies: "You know, I had never met Floyd's (not his real name) wife before. But I met her today and noticed how stunning she is. I was just trying to figure out how Floyd managed to marry such a beautiful woman." At which point one of my friends instantly piped up and said, "Art, that's what we say about you behind your back."

We all laughed. And I had been put in my place. They all knew that I married above myself big-time. (Literally, as Holly is 5'10" and I am 5'8"). Or as I often tell people, I outpunted my coverage in a big way.

Sometimes, we need a piece of humble pie, and I had just eaten a huge slice. Staying connected to the body of Christ provides healthy challenges at just the right times.

Jesus' goal is to get us to see the world upside down. And for us to experience the rewards of living by a new reality. Jesus is an upside-down king. He rules another kingdom. A kingdom not of this world.

The kingdom of God and the kingdom of this world are not just in competition, they are locked in an inverse relationship.

Think again of the example of Albert Schweitzer. He was called on to speak to a group of young people who were getting their medical degrees. He said, "I don't know what your destiny will be. But one thing I do know: The only ones among you who will be really happy are those who have sought, and found how to serve." If you want to find happiness, learn how to serve. If you want to find greatness, go to the bottom of the ladder, instead of the top. Choose reality. Choose to serve God and serve others. Choose the upside-down kingdom. Because it's the only way to real greatness.

John McRay taught at a Christian school. He tells of one of his college students. The student had been dismissed from school but was later readmitted. He had a brilliant mind and a willingness to learn. By the end of the semester, his study about Jesus with Dr. McRay had ignited a flame inside him. He finished at the top of the class and asked to repeat the course the following semester, to study the Greek text. McRay said, "I learned more than I taught. I had found a pearl of great price." McRay wanted him to take a PhD, but the young man and his bride went to the ghettos of New York City to provide remedial education and to teach kids about Christ.

During those months in Brooklyn, the two men corresponded. The student wrote, "Dear Dr. McRay, charis kai eirene (grace and peace). Although our schedule here has been hectic, I have been able to grab a few minutes to continue studying Hebrews." Months later, he sat in McRay's living room in Tennessee. He told how he had been attacked by a gang. A few weeks later, McRay received word that the young man had been shot to death in the stairwell of his Brooklyn apartment. He had refused to ring the doorbell because it would have endangered his wife inside, who was expecting their first child. That is what Christ the servant King will motivate us to do. To give ourselves in life or in death as a sacrifice for others.

LORD OF THE RINGS

The second film in *The Lord of the Rings* trilogy is *The Two Towers*. It's about a group of people who have lost their nerve. They're in denial about the evil that grows closer and closer to their borders. They don't do anything about it until they are backed into a corner, fighting for their lives. But the king's daughter is not like many of the people who have lost their courage. She practices for battle with a large sword. She's small, but she's strong and able. Someone comments on her skill. She says, "The women of our country have had to learn that just because you do not carry a sword does not mean you cannot die upon one. I fear neither death nor pain." Then she is asked, "What do you fear?" She says, "A cage. To stay behind bars until use and old age accept them and all chance of valor has gone beyond recall or desire."

Too many Christians are living in a cage. They are sitting behind bars. They are content to be prisoners of apathy and materialism and self-centeredness. They're in danger of accepting those prison bars. Until all chance of valor has gone. I don't want to live the rest of my life as a prisoner. Do you? I want to live as a servant. I want to step up and say, "I will take the Ring! I will swing the sword! I will be a servant!"

The Poseidon Adventure is a movie about an ocean liner that hits a terrible storm. A wall of water crashes through the ballroom. Men and women in their finery go running for cover. The ship loses power, the lights go out, and the ship lurches over. There is enough air trapped inside to keep the liner floating upside down. But the passengers are in full panic, frantically trying to save their own lives. They're so disoriented they start climbing the stairs to the top deck. The problem is that this deck is now one hundred feet underwater. Scrambling to the top results in death. The only survivors are those who do the opposite. Others rush to their deaths, but a few wiser passengers descend into the dark belly of the ship until they reach the hull. When they reach the bottom, they find the surface of the ocean, the top. Rescuers hear them banging at the hull and cut them free.

"He who saves his life will lose it, but whoever loses his life for My sake will find it."

PRAYER:

"Father, please teach me the paradox of finding greatness through serving. Jesus, show me what it means to emulate your heart of giving. Holy Spirit, lead me to find peace in obscurity, unselfishness, and a willingness to surrender my instinct to go first. Give me the heart of the Father, Son, and Spirit."

PRACTICAL SUGGESTIONS:

1. This week, deliberately choose to take the last place in line. Remember, leaders eat last.
2. Look for some way in which you need to do the opposite of your normal routine, a routine in which you scramble to be at the top.
3. Pay a visit to someone who is 'weak.' An invalid, a homeless person, a special needs person. Ask God to show you what He wants you to learn in the process.

DISCUSSION QUESTIONS:

1. Do you believe Jesus when he says, "He who saves his life will lose it, and he who loses his life will find it."?
2. Read Ephesians 5:18–33. What role does the Holy Spirit play in our learning to submit to others?
3. Is there anyone to whom you are failing to submit?
4. How might you follow Jesus' example in moving to the bottom?

CHAPTER 4

The Power of Second Fiddle

***

Leonard Bernstein was the legendary conductor of the New York Philharmonic Orchestra. He was approached by a reporter one day and asked, "Mr. Bernstein, what is the most difficult instrument to play?" He instantly responded, "Second fiddle. I can get plenty of first violinists, but to find one who plays second violin with as much enthusiasm or second French horn or second flute, now that's a problem. And yet, if no one plays second, we have no harmony."

IN A SELF-DOMINATED CULTURE, IT's hard to find people willing to play second fiddle. And even tougher to find people who are genuinely willing to die to themselves.

Let me give you another little quiz. Respond with the first thing that comes to your mind.

Your boss says there's a shake-up in your company. Things are being reorganized and your job is going away. But the good news is that you get to apply for another position. You can either apply for a promotion or a demotion. Which one would you choose, the promotion or the demotion? Let's say that you get the promotion. This means you have to move to a different office. You have a choice between a bigger office or a smaller office. Which one would you choose, the bigger office or the smaller office?

If we're honest, most of us would say that we almost automatically choose the bigger and better.

Instinctively, we think the way to real life is to reach for more. We think the best way to live is to move up, not down. We love to think about upgrading, and we hate to think about downsizing.

We also tend to think that the best approach to life is to make sure we look out for number one. If our security or safety or status is threatened, our first reflex is to take care of ourselves. But moving up may not be the best strategy after all. Maybe prosperity is a greater threat to our lives than adversity. Maybe moving down is often the healthiest thing you can do with your life.

Leith Anderson went to Manila in the Philippines and saw something shocking. He saw the world's largest garbage dump. It's a dump where tens of thousands of people make their homes.

Shacks are built out of things other people have thrown away. People go out and scavenge for food from other people's garbage so they can have enough to eat. People have been born there and grow up there on the garbage heap. Some people spend their whole lives there: they have their families, their shacks, their garbage to eat, and they die there without ever going anyplace else. But what's amazing is that there are American missionaries who also live in the garbage dump. They have chosen to leave their life of comfort in America and spend their lives on the dump.

Examples like this make most of us squirm. But Jesus won't let us off the hook. He says, "Whoever wants to be my disciple must deny themselves and take up the cross and follow me." (Mark 8:34) I find that daunting. Intimidating. I look for ways to run from service, instead of toward it.

The Gospel of Mark records the attitude of James and John toward service. They come asking for positions of power in Jesus' kingdom. They want to be the secretary of state and the secretary of defense when the new order is established. They don't ask what they can do for the kingdom—they ask what the kingdom can do for them.

Their ask is especially shocking when you think about the context. Jesus has just announced that he's on his way to Jerusalem. Where the religious leaders will mock him and spit on him. Flog him and kill him. And all James and John can think about are the place cards at the banquet. They're still thinking he's headed to Jerusalem to restore the glory of the fallen throne of David. They want places of honor when Jesus rises to power. Jesus has been explicit. But they still don't get it. They're guilty of selective hearing. When they should have been thinking about Christ, all they can think about is themselves.

They may have offered the most selfish prayer ever: "We want you to do for us whatever we ask." They're looking for a blank check. John Stott points out that the purpose of prayer is not to bend God's will to ours but to bend our wills to God's. But sometimes, we live with the ultimate demanding spirit: "Our wish should be your command. We want to walk into the messianic candy store and get whatever we want. So Jesus says, "What do you want me to do for you?" They say, "Let one of us sit at your right and the other at your left in your glory. We want the most prestigious positions in the new cabinet." They're jockeying for power and positions.

You can now buy 'Love Yourself' affirmation cards. If those are not enough, also available are shirts that announce 'I heart ME' or 'Love Yourself.' Parents are being sold on teaching their kids self-admiration. *The Breastfeeding Book,* by Martha and William Sears, notes that one of the benefits of breastfeeding is milder-smelling stools. This is great for parents, but it's good for baby, too: "When the baby looks at the face of the diaper-changing caregiver and sees happiness rather than disgust, he picks up a good message about himself— perhaps a perk for budding self-esteem." As someone has put it, we need to make sure our kids know their poop doesn't stink.

But Jesus counters their request by reminding them that the only genuine leadership is servant leadership. "...whoever wants to become great among you must be your servant, and whoever wants to be first must be slave of all. For even the Son of Man did not come to be served, but to serve, and to give his life as a ransom for many." (Mark 10:44–45)

Roman society was all about power. Threats and intimidation and currying favor. Scrambling for places of honor. Cutthroat competition. Looking out for Number One. If other people got crushed in the process, so be it.

Historian Garret Fagan summarizes how the Romans viewed the values of strength and weakness: "Weak members of society were objects not of compassion but of derision. More than most, Romans lionized strength over weakness, victory over defeat, dominion over obedience. Losers paid a harsh price and got what they deserved, and resisters were to be ruthlessly handled... Roman politics became a ruthless game of total winners and abject losers... The drive to dominate and not be forced to bow before a rival was paramount." It's in this cultural milieu that Jesus says, "Not so with you."[5]

"...Whoever wants to become great among you must be your servant." This is not so much an admonition as it is a description. Jesus is just describing leadership in the kingdom. There's no such thing as leadership apart from service. Leadership without service is a contradiction in terms. If you aspire to be a leader, you have to be a servant. The way up is down. Otherwise, you're not a leader. Your claim to be a leader is bogus.

Jesus uses two different words here that are mind-boggling. First, the word servant or diakonoi. A diakonoi is someone who does menial service. He waits at tables or mops the floors. The word diakonoi describes service in terms of function. But the second word is even more explosive. It's the word doulos, which means slave. Doulos described servanthood in terms of position. A slave was under his master. A slave did whatever his master told him to do. Jesus identified the slave as the greatest person. It would have seemed like an oxymoron to the disciples.

But just to make sure the disciples get the point, Jesus says, "...even the Son of Man did not come to be served, but to serve, and to give his life as a ransom for many." The word ransom is crucial. Jesus will not only be a servant, but he will give his life for people held hostage by sin. Jesus will make a payment that no one else can make. He is the suffering servant of Isaiah 53 who will die for the sins of the people.

WE HAVE A CHOICE

We have a choice between selfish ambition and sacrifice. James and John wanted to vie for the best seats. They wanted to make advance reservations. Their attitude is represented in our culture of competition. A culture that urges us to be status seekers, hungry for prestige.

We have a choice between power and service. James and John are looking for thrones. They probably came from a well-to-do family. Their father, Zebedee, had employees in his fishing business, so maybe they were used to having people wait on them, serve them. They were power-mongers making a power play.

We have a choice between comfort and suffering. James and John were daydreaming about a kingdom banquet where they would take it easy and live in luxury. They wanted to drink cups of wine at the messianic banquet. But Jesus throws all of that out. He says the kingdom is not about a cushy life but a cross-filled life.

It's easy for us to roll our eyes at James and John and think, *How could those guys be so selfish? How could they let their ambition get in the way of the kingdom?* But we all have our own issues with ambition.

Too often, I'm like James and John. I look for ways to work a room to my benefit. I find ways to ingratiate myself with others who can do something to my advantage. I look for convenient excuses to bypass service. I search for God's approval for my ambition. I look for ways to make a name for myself instead of promoting the name of Christ. Self-promotion and servanthood don't mix. And servants think of ministry as an opportunity, not an obligation.

There's something in us that loves things that are glorious. Paul Tripp points out that we are all 'glory junkies.' "Admit it. You're a glory junkie. That's why you like the 360-degree between-the-legs slam dunk or that amazing hand-beaded formal gown or the seven-layer triple-chocolate mousse cake. It's why you're attracted to the hugeness of a mountain range or the multi-hued splendor of the sunset. You were hardwired by your Creator for a glory orientation. It is inescapable. It's in your genes."

Glory stirs something inside us. We're stunned with the majesty of the Rockies or the dunking ability of Lebron James or the genius of a virtuoso performance. And here's the irony: God is not opposed to glory. But God recognizes that all glory begins and ends with him. And any time we seek to glorify ourselves, glory is compromised, and ambition is corrupted.

GOD IS GLORIOUS IN HIMSELF

Psalm 66:1-2: Shout for joy to God, all the earth. Sing the glory of his name; make his praise glorious.

Psalm 145:3: Great is the LORD and most worthy of praise; his greatness no one can fathom.

Psalm 148:13: Let them praise the name of the LORD, for his name alone is exalted; his splendor is above the earth and the heavens.

Jesus as the Son of God is the personification of the glory of God.

2 Corinthians 4:6: "…the light of the gospel of the glory of God, in the face of Jesus Christ."

Hebrews 1:3: He is the radiance of the glory of God.

The problem is that man decided to pursue his own glory instead of the glory of God. Where did Satan come from? Satan is a fallen angel who coveted the glory of God. He is obsessed with stealing glory away from God. His 24/7 pursuit is to grab glory from God. So, he formulated a strategy for doing just that. He lied to Adam and Eve in the garden. He brainwashed them to believe that they would be happier if they received the glory instead of God receiving the glory. He contaminated their minds to buy into the myth that they deserved the glory instead of giving the glory to God. That's the history of mankind in a nutshell. We want to pirate away the glory that belongs only to God.

The Bible has a word for this compulsion to seek our own glory: selfish ambition. Galatians 5:22 lists it as one of the acts of the sinful nature. James 3:16 reminds us, "For where jealousy and selfish ambition exist, there will be disorder and every vile practice."

Dave Harvey gives some of his titles for greatness in his own campaign for personal glory:

Dave the Great in His Own Mind: "This Dave thinks great thoughts—about Dave. He has wonderful plans—for Dave. He can always think of a way to do it better than the other guy. He's ready to offer his valuable opinion about anything. Just ask. Sometimes you don't even need to ask; his opinions just topple out like golden nuggets from an overstuffed treasure chest."

Dave the Comparatively Great: "This Dave is always a seven out of ten. Not perfect, but certainly better than average. Dave the Comparatively Great is extremely conscious of the competition. He knows what it takes to stay ahead of the average guy. This Dave doesn't appreciate somebody being promoted over him. It messes up his comparison index. He loves to win, hates to lose."

Dave the I'll be Great If It Kills Me: "This Dave is so motivated for greatness that he's fixated on his goals. He pushes hard and won't take no for an answer. Failure's just not an option."[6]

Your push for glory may take different forms. But at the core, we've all been corrupted by a desire to promote ourselves instead of promoting God. This is the central issue of sin—denying the glory of God and reaching for our own glory. Paul gives a description of the downward spiral of sin: "For although they knew God, they neither glorified him as God nor gave thanks to him, but their thinking became futile, and their foolish hearts were darkened." (Romans 1:21)

But here's the good news: God acted to save us from our selfish quest for glory.

First, Jesus paid the price for our self-seeking grabs for glory. That's what Jesus means in Mark 10:45. He will give his life as a ransom for many. Why did we need a ransom? Because we were held hostage by our hell-bent quest for glory. We were consumed by a desire to swipe glory from God and claim it for ourselves. But then Jesus came. He absorbed the holy wrath of God against sin. He paid the ransom that makes us free.

Second, Jesus lived a perfect life so that your standing before God is perfect. It is not just that your sin is paid for and erased. It is that the perfection of Christ is credited to your account. Not only are there no debts, but your account is also credited with the flawless record of the Son of God.

To appreciate the value of forfeiting our insistence on glorifying ourselves, think about the critical importance of selflessness in marriage. Selfishness is the single biggest destroyer of marriages. If I approach my wife, Holly, with an attitude that it's all about me, it's devastating. I have to die to self. This means giving up my so-called 'rights.' This means giving up my preferences.

If I'm self-focused, I'll see everything through the lens of me. "What about me? Nobody's gonna step on me." But when I die to myself, it changes everything. I'll volunteer to help in the kitchen and initiate helping with the kids. I'll ask, "What would please her?" instead of asking, "What would please me?" I'll ask, "What would Jesus do in this situation?" Jesus was clear. "If anyone desires to come after Me, let him deny himself, and take up his cross daily, and follow Me." (Luke 9: 23)

My mother was paralyzed after a surgery gone bad many years ago. For the next eight years, my dad took care of her. He bought a van equipped with a place for a motorized wheelchair. Mom clicked a remote which launched a ramp on the side of the van, allowing her to 'drive' the wheelchair up into the passenger side. Dad then used a series of pullies and metal hooks to lock Mom's chair into place. And that was just a small aspect of his service to her. He helped Mom get dressed, helped prepare her meals, and emptied her catheter. He did all of this without complaining even once. He was the definition of a servant. He demonstrated the power of weakness in ways I'll never forget.

Think about the legacy we are leaving our children. Tom Farrey wrote a book called *Game On: The All-American Race to Make Champions of Our Children*. Farrey warns parents about the excessive pressure they can put on their kids to succeed.

> There are 12-year-olds driving race cars. Eleven-year-olds are turning pro in skateboarding. Nine-year-olds hire professional coaches. Eight-year-olds play 75 baseball games a year. Seven-year-olds vie for power-lifting medals. Six-year-olds have personal trainers. Five-year-olds play soccer year-round. Four-year-old tumblers compete at the AAU Junior Olympics. Three-year-olds enter their third year of swim lessons. Two-year-olds have custom gold clubs. Just for kicks, to get a sense for where all this might be headed, I flew to Australia with a cheek swab from my one-year-old son, Kellen, to get his DNA tested by a company that uses genetic analysis to recommend specific sports. Guess what? My baby boy has the right stuff for a specific Winter Olympic event.[7]

The problem is that we sometimes nudge our kids to be ambitious in every area except the one area that matters most: the kingdom of God. Of course, if our kids are going to learn what servant leadership is about, it starts with us. Values are more caught than taught.

When our children were young, my wife, Holly, would take them almost every week to visit someone in need. The visits were often with Don and Glenna Barnes. Glenna had suffered a serious illness and lived most of her days in a wheelchair. Don was in his nineties, and even though still healthy, needed help in caring for Glenna. Our girls watched as Holly ministered to the Barnes, taking meals or running errands or whatever needed to be done. Holly was living out the meaning of the power of weakness.

Philippians 2:3–4: "Do nothing out of selfish ambition or vain conceit. Rather, in humility consider others better than yourselves, not looking to your own interests but also to the interests of others."

1 John 3:16: "This is how we know what love is: Jesus Christ laid down his life for us. And we ought to lay down our lives for our brothers and sisters."

I have witnessed remarkable examples of service to others.

A few years ago, while on a mission trip to Russia, I met a young mother whose daughter had been born with the lower half of her left leg missing. The little girl was vibrant and happy but faced a lifetime of serious disability. Members of our church, Tom and Margaret Kincannon, had come to know the mother and daughter and arranged for both to fly to Dallas, where the little girl could be examined for potential surgery.

After receiving a request from the Kincannons, the Shriner's Hospital in Dallas agreed to do the procedure, which enabled the little girl to receive a prosthesis that dramatically improved her quality of life. Tom and Margaret personified the spirit of Christ in seeking out the weak.

I read about a man who had completely submitted himself to a leader. The leader, to teach the submitted person servanthood, required that person to mow the leader's lawn. That is a reversal of the Jesus style. The leader should have mowed the protégé's lawn.

Leadership means being part of the secret service. I have a friend who exhibits this quality. He has made millions in his life and gives away most of what he earns to help others. He has developed a special trust designed to resource people in need. I can't imagine how much money he has given away over the years. But he insists on his gifts being anonymous. He refuses to let his generosity be known. Most of us can serve with passion in the event there's some 'payoff' in terms of recognition. But how many of us bring the same enthusiasm to opportunities to serve behind the scenes? Where nobody sees and nobody knows?

1 Peter 2:12: "Live such good lives among the pagans that, though they accuse you of doing wrong, they may see your good deeds and glorify God on the day he visits us."

THE HEROD SYNDROME

Do you remember what happened when Jesus was born? King Herod got wind of the news about a new king being born. Herod was insanely jealous. He couldn't tolerate the thought of a rival. He was manic about holding on to his power. So he sent his henchmen and had all the baby boys in Bethlehem murdered. But we all live with the Herod syndrome. Herod lives in all of us.

It's a perspective that says, *I don't want anyone else to be king. I want to occupy the throne of my life and do whatever I want to do.* So we try to make ourselves the center of the story. Think about how short our lives are. We're part of a movie for a split second in the drama of history. We're bit players in an epic story in which Christ is the star. Still, we sometimes think the movie is about us. We crown ourselves instead of Christ.

God doesn't exist to make much of you. You exist to make much of God. You were divinely designed to bring glory to God. God's priority is to reveal himself and make himself known. This trumps your comfort, your personal preferences, your desires—anything that might come before God in your life. So Christ is calling you to dethrone yourself and enthrone Christ as the ruler of your life. Christ has every right to do that. Because He is the King who went to the cross.

Jesus was maybe the least likely king in history. He was a king with no pride or prestige. He refused to covet the plaudits of the crowd. He came riding into Jerusalem on a donkey instead of a spirited stallion. It was his very humility that resulted in his exaltation!

PRAYER:

"Father, show me your will for my life. Thank you for never calling me without equipping me. Give me a spirit of discernment so I can know which spiritual gifts you want me to utilize. Help me be a conduit of blessing to others by surrendering my preferences and chasing after your direction. Use me today in a powerful way as I choose the path of powerlessness."

PRACTICAL SUGGESTIONS:

1. This week, look at these passages about spiritual gifts:
   Romans 12:6–8
   1 Corinthians 12:4–31
   Ephesians 4:11
   1 Peter 4:10–11
   Ask God to show you the gifts he has given you. Then ask him to show you the corresponding ministry in which he wants you to use your gifts.
2. Do something to serve someone that will help defuse your ego.

DISCUSSION QUESTIONS:

1. What spiritual gifts do you believe God has given you through the Holy Spirit? How are you exercising those gifts?
2. What is the greatest gift from the Holy Spirit? (1 Corinthians 13:1–7)
3. What makes it difficult for you to serve others?
4. Spend time as a group praying that God will help you demonstrate the love of Christ to others.

CHAPTER 5

Weakness is the New Strength

✳✳✳

My grace is sufficient for you, for my power is made perfect in weakness.

—Jesus to the apostle Paul

A MINISTER GOT A CALL from a young man he had known a few years before. The young man's name was Tim Vanderveen. Tim had graduated from Hope College. He was tall, broad-shouldered, and handsome. But then he developed leukemia. The minister went to see Tim in the hospital. Tim's mother was sitting in the corner crying. Tim was lying on his side. Pillows were positioned between his skinny legs. Tim didn't have enough energy to look up. The minister got down on one knee so he could look into his eyes. He said, "Hi, Tim." There was an awkward silence.

Then Tim said, "I've learned something." The minister said, "Tell me, partner, what have you learned?" "I have learned that you can't fast forward through the bad parts. But I have learned that Jesus Christ is in every frame, and right now, that's just enough." Tim hated what he was going through, but he experienced the presence of Christ in the middle of his hurt. He knew God's grace was sufficient. And when Tim breathed his last breath here on Earth, God's grace was sufficient.

Think right now of some hurt in your life. Or some trouble that might be waiting for you out there. Do you realize that God's grace is sufficient? Do you realize God will never let you go through anything without giving you the grace to handle it? Paul said, "I can do all things through Christ who strengthens me." (Philippians 4:13) It doesn't make any difference how huge the hurt is: God will give you the grace to clear any hurdle.

That's the message God gave Paul. Paul begged God three times to take away his weakness. "But he said, 'My grace is sufficient for you…'" It wasn't the answer Paul wanted, but it was the answer he needed. By the way, the verb, 'God said' is in the perfect tense. It means something that happened in the past continues to be evident in the present. Paul can still hear God's answer echoing in his ears. What God said to Paul in the past is a tremendous assurance in the present. Because he knows he can deal with anything by the power of God's grace.

I talked with a man who lost his six-year-old son to cancer. I asked him to tell me about it. He said, "It was amazing to see how God gave our family the strength we needed during that nightmare." He told me about people he met and the power he received to bear up under the heartache and the hurt. He said, "God's grace was with us all the way through."

Sometimes we ask God to take away the thorn and he doesn't. And we think maybe God hasn't answered. But we may discover that the answer is more profound than anything we know to ask from God. God doesn't always deliver us from the pain, but he always gives us grace to deal with the pain. Remember, these things didn't happen to Paul because he was *out* of God's will but because he was *in* God's will. God wanted to do something even greater in Paul. Philip Brooks said, "I do not ask for tasks equal to my powers: I ask for powers equal to my tasks."

God said, "My grace is sufficient." It means complete. It means you can be content no matter how tough things become. You can reach a place in life where nothing else in the world can make you complete except God. He's more than enough in your life. God is teaching you that you can lack the things you think you need but still be totally content.

God's people have always discovered that his grace is sufficient. Stephen was stoned to death, but God's grace was sufficient. The

Macedonian believers faced extreme poverty, but God's grace was sufficient. John died in exile on a barren island, but God's grace was sufficient. Jerusalem Christians were hounded from their homes, but God's grace provided for their needs. Many early Christians were slaves. Some were women with unbelieving husbands who didn't understand them. Some were singles, longing to get married but afraid to marry in uncertain times. Many were sick and persecuted for their faith. But God's grace was sufficient.

God's grace carried them through the darkest nights of their lives. You can go through broken relationships, broken promises, and broken expectations, but you don't have to become a broken person. Pain is inevitable, misery is optional. Grace is not just God's saving power. Grace is God's sustaining power. His grace is sufficient for your weakness.

Joni Tada was paralyzed as a teenager in a diving accident. Listen to Joni's words about one of her experiences in life.

Honesty is always the best policy, especially when you are surrounded by women in a restroom during a break at a Christian women's conference. One woman, putting on lipstick, said, "Oh, Joni, you always look so together, so happy in your wheelchair. I wish that I had your joy!" Several women around me nodded. "How do you do it?" she asked as she capped her lipstick.

"I don't do it," I said. "May I tell you honestly how I woke up this morning? This is an average day. After my husband, Ken, leaves for work at 6:00 a.m., I'm alone until I hear the front door open at 7:00 a.m. That's when a friend arrives to get me up. While she makes coffee, I pray, 'Lord, my friend will soon give me a bath, get me dressed, sit me up in my chair, brush my hair and teeth, and send me out the door. I don't have the strength to face this routine one more time. I have no resources. I don't have a smile to take into the day. But you do. May I have yours? God, I need you desperately.'"

"So what happens when your friend comes into the bedroom?" one of them asked.

"I turn my head toward her and give her a smile sent straight from heaven. It's not mine; it's God's." I point to my paralyzed legs. "Whatever joy you see today was hard won this morning. **I have learned that the weaker we are, the more we need to lean on God; and the more we lean on God, the stronger we find him to be.**"[8]

"My grace is sufficient for you, for my power is made perfect in weakness." Paul didn't just receive grace to deal with trouble. He received power through it. Paul's thorn cut him down to size. It kept him in touch with his limitations. It reminded him that he was powerless without God. *Weakness is a prerequisite for God's power.* If you're self-sufficient, you'll never experience the flow of God's power in your life.

This can lead us to convince ourselves that God can only use us if we are robust and independent and able.

Can I challenge you to let God use you in your weakness? It's enticing to think we can do little for God if we're weak. It's tempting to hide behind excuses for not attempting good things for God. "I'm not very good at teaching." "I'm scared when I think about sharing my faith: I don't know how to talk to people." "I'm not a good writer." "I don't have a strong personality." "I don't have many gifts." "I don't have the talent to start a ministry for God." "My track record is sullied and marked with failure, so I think I'll sit on the sidelines." We forget that his power is made perfect in weakness.

CHUCK COLSON

Chuck Colson came to understand the power of weakness. His career had been established on the basis of power and preeminence. He had worked in the Oval Office and held enormous prestige. After going to prison following Watergate, he had resigned himself to never accomplishing anything. But he finally came to the end of himself. With God's help, he launched a prison ministry that has introduced thousands of inmates to Christ.

> "The great paradox [of my life] is that every time I walk into a prison and see the faces of men or women who have been transformed by the power of the living God, I realize that the thing God has chosen to use in my life… is none of the successes, achievements, degrees, awards, honors, or cases I won before the Supreme Court. That's not what God's using in my life. What God is using in my life to touch the lives of literally thousands of other people is the fact that I was a convict and went to prison. That was my great defeat, the only thing in my life I didn't succeed in."[9]

WHEN YOU ARE MOST BROKEN

When you're most broken, God may be ready to do his strongest work. God always builds his kingdom on weakness. Never on strength. God doesn't use you *in spite of* your weakness but *through* your weakness. Think of all the things you think make you unqualified for ministry: your struggles, your battles, your inabilities. But all the things you think make you unqualified actually make you qualified.

God always works through the little people. Think about the people Jesus used for great things: outcasts and foreigners and people who were weak. God always does his biggest work in the littlest of people. So, if you think you don't have much to offer, think again. The irony is, God does his greatest work in people who are weak.

I was watching TV one day when I saw a very unusual preacher. He didn't speak clearly. You could tell he had a speech defect. Some of his words were garbled. He twisted his mouth when he talked. But it was one of the most powerful messages I'd ever heard. His name is David Ring. He has cerebral palsy. He wanted to be a preacher, but people told him he'd never make it as a preacher. He went on to preach in over 200 churches a year. He inspired everyone who heard him preach. His most famous message was called 'I've Got Cerebral Palsy—What's Your Problem?' He told people that they had no excuse for not serving Christ. Because God uses the weakest people to do the biggest things. Now let me ask you: He has cerebral palsy. What's your problem? He didn't let cerebral palsy keep him from telling other people about Jesus. What's your excuse?

Don't ever let your weakness get in the way of serving God. The people reading this book who will do the most for God are the people who know their weaknesses. If we could somehow look into the future and see the people who will make the biggest impact for God, they would be the people we think of as least likely to make a mark for God.

His power is made perfect in weakness. Paul believed this right down to his toes. He says, "That is why, for Christ's sake, I delight in weaknesses, in insults, in hardships, in persecutions, in difficulties. For when I am weak, then I am strong." (2 Corinthians 12:10)

> Here's the formula: Depending on God + admitting your weaknesses = your weaknesses being transformed into his strengths

Paul isn't stoic about his pain. He doesn't like it. But he's actually reached a place where he celebrates his suffering. Because he knows his weakness is the occasion for God's strength. He knows that God always works through weakness. So what does that mean for us? It means that instead of being defeated by weakness, we look for the ways God can use our weakness to do good things. It means we ask God to help us get over our self-sufficiency. Maybe you're like me: often, the motto of my life has often been, "I can do it myself. I can handle this." I suspect many of you can relate to that.

THE POWER OF ADMITTING WEAKNESS

There's power in admitting our weakness. If you go to an AA meeting, the first step is to admit that you're powerless. The reality is, we're all powerless. We're all weak. But we have to admit our weakness.

A BIZARRE ORDER

Do you know the story of Gideon? The people of Israel have lived under the tyranny of the Midianites for seven years. The people cry out for help. God says, "Gideon, I'll use you to overcome the enemy." Gideon says, **"But Lord, how can I save Israel? My clan is the weakest in Manasseh, and I am the least in my family"** (Judges 6:15) Do you see what God is doing? God is about to show Gideon that his power is always made perfect in weakness. Later, the time comes for battle. Gideon calls his troops together, and he has 32,000 men. But God says, Gideon, "I want you to thin the ranks. That's too many troops. If you go into battle with that many men, you'll think you've won the battle. So cut down on the number of your troops." So 22,000 men went home, and now, Gideon had 10,000 men.

But God said, "Gideon that's still too many men. I want you to take your men down to the water." Then God had Gideon do a strange thing. He said, "Your men are going to drink water in two different ways." By the way, I think you see God's sense of humor here. God says, "Some of your men will lap water with their tongues, like a dog. And some of your guys will scoop up water into their hands and drink that way. Now I want you to take the guys who scoop up water with their hands and use them for your army."

Only 300 men scoop up water with their hands. God says, "That's all the men you get. You can only use 300 men to fight the Midianites." Now why would God do it this way? Judges 7:3 has the answer: "In order that Israel may not boast against me that her own strength has saved her..." Gideon finally realized he couldn't do *anything* until he trusted *everything* to God.

We're tempted to try to save ourselves. But the Bible says we're impotent in the face of our challenges. **"You see, at just the right time, when we were still powerless, Christ died for the ungodly."** (Romans 5:6) We were defenseless against the guilt and power of sin. Completely at the mercy of our sinful nature. So God stepped in and did what we could never do.

Our culture is saturated with books and seminars on self-help. There's nothing intrinsically wrong with self-help, of course. But we need to resist the enticing call of a culture that teaches us we are defined by our relationship to self, instead of to God. We must recognize the inherent limitations of the self-help movement. We need the Holy Spirit to remind us of our dependence on God. So, ask God to give you the reminders you need to avoid self-reliance and to depend on him for the needs of every moment in every day.

NOT IN YOUR OWN STRENGTH

You can never do anything for God if you rely on your own strength. You have to be willing to let God break you. You have to say, "God, I'm completely helpless without you." When you finally reach the place where you know you don't have any strength, his strength is released. He wants us to be weak so there will be room in our lives for his strength.

Just think what would happen if you decided today to stop relying on your own strength and to start relying only on God's strength? What would happen if you started praying like you've never prayed before? God would give you victories you can't even begin to imagine.

Dave Dravecky was a star pitcher for the San Francisco Giants. Then he lost one of his arms to cancer. He said, "In America, Christians pray for the burden of suffering to be lifted from their backs. In the rest of the world, Christians pray for stronger backs so they can bear their suffering. It's why we look away from the bag lady and to the displays in store windows. Why we prefer going to the movies instead of to hospitals and nursing homes."

We're uncomfortable with the way of weakness, the way of the cross. The cross is a scandal in a me-first culture. Most people covet power and success and wealth. Anything but a cross. The message of the cross is too hideous for most people to hear. Most want to hear about how God sanctifies success. If you just follow Jesus, you'll be healthy and wealthy, and everything will be good in your life.

So the question is, have you accepted the message of the cross? Are you living for success or surrender? Are you living for your career or for Christ? What is the highest value in your life? Just be honest about that for a minute. Don't dismiss it. Answer the question. And if you're not living for the cross, what will you do to change that?

In the movie *Braveheart*, William Wallace says, "Every man dies. Not every man really lives." If you live for anyone other than Christ, you don't really have a life. When a believer loses his job but responds with trust and perseverance, the life of Christ seeps through. When a Christ-follower finds herself flat on her back in a hospital bed but blesses the people around her with grace and faith, the life of Christ spills out. When people celebrate a person's life at the funeral of a Christian, the life of Christ fills the room with the aroma of Christ.

Surrender your troubles to God's grace. Trust that God will give you the grace to handle any hurt. Don't be intimidated by any troubles. Remember that God will never let you go through anything without also giving you the power to deal with it. His grace really is enough to carry you through.

Celebrate your troubles in the light of God's grace. Remember that God always works through broken people to accomplish his purposes. When somebody insults you at work, remember his power is made perfect in weakness. When you go through hardships, remember his power is made perfect in weakness. When the walls are caving in, remember his power is made perfect in weakness.

Don't ever underestimate the power of weakness. Jesus lived his whole life in weakness. He died in a helpless heap on a shameful cross.

People said, "What a pitiful, pathetic picture of weakness." But it was his very weakness that produced his power. Power over sin and death in the resurrection. The power to change your life. Remember: His grace is sufficient for you. His power is made perfect in weakness.

PRAYER:

"Father, I am often blind to the power of weakness. I choose to resent my weakness instead of embracing what you are able to do through my weakness. Help me identify the ways in which you want to leverage my weakness for your strength. Show me how it is that you may employ my weakness for your glory. Help me to celebrate your ability to transcend my weakness and turn it into something good for you."

PRACTICAL SUGGESTIONS:

1. Find someone who has been afflicted with a disability or an especially tough challenge in her life, but who lives with exceptional courage. Interview her and ask her to detail her walk with Christ.
2. Ask God to show you how your 'thorn' can be used for his glory. Ask the Holy Spirit to guide you in this.

DISCUSSION QUESTIONS:

1. Do you have a 'thorn in the flesh'? How has that affected your life? Do you believe there's anything you have learned from it?
2. How might a challenge in your life make you more effective for Christ?
3. Read Hebrews 12:1–13. How is Christ our inspiration as we go through adversity?
4. What value is there in discipline from God?

CHAPTER 6

The Power of Cracked Pots

***

God comes in where my helplessness begins.

—Oswald Chambers

WHEN I WAS FIVE YEARS old, our family moved from southwest Missouri to the sprawling city of Kansas City. After about a year, we moved back to what would become our permanent hometown of Springfield. By then, I was six years old and attending first grade at Bingham Elementary. At recess, we went out to the field to play softball. My limited sports experience in Kansas City consisted of nothing but dodgeball, so I had never swung a bat.

My poor skills proved to be devastating. I would strike out every time I came to bat. Other kids made fun of the fact that I fanned at every pitch. Some kids wanted to take my 'third strike' so that maybe a strikeout wouldn't be inevitable. I was often picked last when sides were chosen. I was hurt and occasionally brought to tears.

My folks looked for help. My grandmother (my mom's mother) would kindly stand in our backyard and toss pitches my way to improve my hitting. I never became a slugger, but over time, I became a better hitter.

I do think this had an impact on my self-esteem. From that point forward, I believe I was determined to prove myself. I never again wanted to be in a position where I was discounted or made fun of. I don't want to exaggerate the result of this experience, but I'm convinced it left a psychological mark that wasn't easily overcome. I'm still working on this. I can try to prove my worth by looking to the opinions of others to validate myself.

Can you relate? How do you feel when you lose the game or lose the corner office or your neighbor is awarded with the 'Yard of the Month'?

It's easy to let Satan sell us the lie that our worth is defined by how we stack up against others. Satan attacks our identity, telling us that others determine our worth, instead of Christ announcing our worth. So we start thinking, *One more like, one more win, and I'll know I'm significant.* But remember, if you use the world's tools to assess your worth, your measurements will always be off. The cross is the measure of your ultimate worth and value.

THE CENTRAL ISSUE OF OUR IDENTITY

Jane Elliott was a schoolteacher in rural Iowa decades ago, during the time that Martin Luther King was assassinated. She wanted to teach her students a lesson on what racism and discrimination do. So, she walked into class one day and announced that brown-eyed students were smarter than blue-eyed students. She moved the brown-eyed students to the front of the classroom, gave them extra recess time, and showed them more favor. She gave the blue-eyed students special collars to wear so that everyone could see from a distance that they were inferior. The next day, she told the students that she had been mistaken. That blue-eyed students were actually smarter than brown-eyed students. All the blue-eyed kids tore off their collars.

It was amazing to see how the students' perception of their identity affected them. When the blue-eyed students wore the collars, they needed an average of 5.5 minutes to complete a reading assignment. But when they got to take off the collars, they did the same exercise in an average of 2.5 minutes. When they had to wear the collars, they reported feeling sad and down. Their understanding of their identity made a big difference in how they lived.[10]

The apostle Paul understood the key to a healthy identity. He realized that he could not allow other people to define him. Paul was clear that his worth was not determined by other people—it was determined by Christ. He was also crystal clear about one other thing—his worth was not determined by strength but by weakness.

Remember, God's power is made perfect in weakness. But sometimes, the slings and arrows of other people leave us feeling completely defeated. Maybe that's one of the reasons we're tempted to assert ourselves. We want to establish ourselves, prove that we are somebody. We've considered the value of Paul's thorn in the flesh. But now I want you to think about another thorn in Paul's life—the thorn of other people who were attacking his ministry.

PAUL'S OTHER THORN: PEOPLE!

Paul feels overwhelmed. He's been through hardships in Asia. He doesn't give us the details. But he says he was under great pressure. We know Paul had been in prison, flogged, stoned, shipwrecked, robbed, starved, and abandoned. Whatever it was, it was intense. So severe that he says, "…in our hearts we felt the sentence of death." (2 Corinthians 1:9)

GETTING KICKED WHEN YOU'RE DOWN

Paul knew what it was to be disappointed and depressed. To feel like giving up. Now, he has another challenge with some of the Corinthians. They're kicking him while he's down. False apostles have wormed their way into the Corinthian church. They attack Paul's motives. And his abilities. And his authority. Paul feels discredited. Has that ever happened to you? You invest your life in someone, and the payback you get is criticism. You do all you can to help someone, and then all they want to do is take shots at you.

Paul comes to Corinth, and the people are not impressed. Paul is not a great speaker like Ronald Reagan. He doesn't have the charisma of a John Kennedy. He's a little man, and he doesn't exactly take over a room when he walks in. So, some of his opponents say, "Paul, you're not an apostle. There's nothing impressive about you or your message." Paul's reaction is amazing. He says, "You're right. I'm not much to look at or listen to. But here's the thing: it's my very weakness that proves the credibility of my witness. I'm so weak, it's obvious that God has to be the power behind my ministry."

God gives Paul the okay to be vulnerable, to be real, and to expose his weaknesses. He's the perfect example of a leader with weaknesses. One of the hardest things to do in life is tell somebody your weaknesses. We think we have to walk around always on point, on top of the world when we're in front of others. We work to assert our strength and independence.

PAUL'S COUNTERINTUITIVE DEFENSE

Paul is not just being 'unfollowed'—he is under severe attack. He's getting dissed. But he doesn't take the criticism sitting down. He's embarrassed to do it, but he knows he has to take up for himself. *It's how he defends himself that might seem bizarre to us. Instead of talking about his strengths, he talks about his weaknesses. His defense is counterintuitive.* Paul argues, "I'm nothing but a cracked pot." Imagine applying for a job, and instead of listing your strengths, you list your weaknesses. Instead of listing your credentials, you talk about your foibles. Instead of rushing to your Facebook page to boost your reputation, you choose not to post anything at all. Or even to list all of your weaknesses.

Consider the word 'weakness' in 1 Corinthians. Because it runs like a thread all the way through Paul's letter. Paul opens with these words: "For the foolishness of God is wiser than man's wisdom, and the weakness of God is stronger than man's strength." (1 Corinthians 1:25). And then, when he talks about spiritual gifts in chapter 12, he says, "Those parts of the body that seem to be weaker are indispensable." (1 Corinthians 12:22) We think the big shots are important in the church. Paul says it's just the opposite.

"But we have this treasure in jars of clay, to show that this all-surpassing power is from God and not from us." (2 Corinthians 4:7) Now the treasure here is the gospel, the good news of Jesus. And the jars of clay are us. Why would God put his treasure in old clay pots? I went to Greece. I saw priceless vessels. I saw beautiful Grecian urns crafted with unbelievable detail. I saw bronze bowls and cups. Museum quality pieces.

CRACKED POTS

But I also saw jars of clay. Earthenware jars. Clay pots. Cheap pottery. Jars of clay are fragile. They're easily chipped or cracked or broken. There's nothing fancy about jars of clay. They're disposable and so cheap, when they break, nobody tries to put them back together.

The actual word used here for jars of clay is ostraca. The Greeks would break off a piece of an old clay pot, and they would write on it. When they considered somebody a threat to democracy, they would ostracize him. Using ostraca. They would write the name of the person being ostracized on a piece of ostraca. Like little ballots. A piece of ostraca was so thin and fragile, you could even write on it.

Paul says, "I'm a cracked pot. I'm fragile, I'm plain, and I'm disposable." By the way, this isn't false modesty. Tradition says Paul was a short man. With a bald head and a crooked nose. Paul was nothing to look at. He showed the effect of all the beatings and shipwrecks and heartaches in his life. Paul had a frail, pummeled body. But Paul's weakness was an occasion for God's strength. This proved that his extraordinary power came from God and not from himself. All of his suffering was part of God's design to spread the good news about Christ.

We are cracked pots. It isn't that we're worthless. We're actually even more valuable because of the treasure that's in us. But the paradox is that God chooses fragile, weak people to get his message across. Paul put it this way: "God chose the foolish things of the world to shame the wise: God chose the weak things of the world to shame the strong, the lowly things of this world and the despised things—and the things that are not—to nullify the things that are." (1 Corinthians 1:27)

Paul goes on to talk about how God uses his weakness to get things done. His words should be a bumper sticker for anyone who's discouraged today. "We are hard pressed on every side, but not crushed; perplexed, but not in despair, persecuted, but not abandoned, struck down, but not destroyed." (2 Corinthians 4:8)

Can you relate to that? Do you ever feel like everyone's out to get you, to make your life difficult? You've been through one setback after another: financial trouble, health problems, the loss of your job, family struggles. Paul had been struck down, stressed out, mixed up, picked on, and knocked down.

But he says this: "We always carry around in our body the death of Jesus, so that the life of Jesus may also be revealed in our body. For we who are alive are always being given over to death for Jesus' sake, so that his life may be revealed in our mortal body. So then, death is at work in us, but life is at work in you." (2 Corinthians 4:10–12)

DYING FOR OTHERS

A few years ago, Christians in the Congo celebrated the hundredth anniversary of the coming of the missionaries to that part of Africa. An old man stood before the crowd. He said that when the missionaries arrived, his people thought they were strange, and their message was dubious. The tribal leaders decided to test the missionaries by slowly poisoning them to death. Over time, the missionary children died one by one. Then, the old man said, "It was as we watched how they died that we decided we wanted to live as Christians." The missionaries who died painful deaths never knew why they were dying or what the impact of their lives and deaths would be. But through it all, they didn't leave. Death was at work in them, but life was at work in the people of the Congo.

Do you realize that when you die for others, you give them life? Jesus said, "Unless a grain of wheat falls into the earth and dies, it remains alone. But if it dies, it bears much fruit." (John 12:24) The physical principle is that when a grain of wheat dies, it multiplies. The spiritual principle is that when we die for Christ, his influence multiplies.

PASSION TO BE NUMBER 1

Robert X Cringely, in his book *Accidental Empires*, talks about the early days of Apple. In the late 1970s, Apple had grown beyond the point that all the employees knew each other on sight. So, it was decided that, like grown-up companies, they should all have name badges. As is the corporate way, it was deemed that these badges should be numbered, and as corporate lore decrees, the number assigned would be based on the order in which employees had joined the company. Cringely writes:

> Steve Wozniak was declared employee number 1. Steve Jobs was number 2, and so on. Jobs didn't want to be number 2. He didn't want to be second in anything. Jobs argued that he, rather than Woz, should have the sacred number one since they were co-founders of the company and J came before W in the alphabet. When that plan was rejected. he argued that the number 0 was still unassigned, and since 0 came before 1, Jobs would be happy to take that number. He got it.

Paul says that we're being given over to death. It's the same expression the gospels use to describe Jesus being turned over to the authorities to be flogged and crucified. Jesus' death resulted in our life. When we're given over to death, it produces life in others. That's true for Paul. Death is chiseling away and breaking him down. But it's producing life in other people. He's willing to die every day. Had he played it safe, they never would have heard of Christ.

Years ago, Holly and I traveled to her parents' home on the west coast. We stayed in the upstairs bedroom, and through the window, we spotted a hummingbird nest. When we first arrived, we could see a tiny nest, no bigger than half an eggshell, perched in the tree outside the window. You could barely see two baby hummingbirds, each about the size of my little finger. The mother would make dozens of trips to the nest during the day. You could see her flapping her wings seventy times per second. And you could also see her dropping little bugs into the babies' mouths.

Actually, she wasn't just dropping the bugs in. She was cramming them down the throats of her little babies. The babies were clutching on so tight that their little bodies just kept bobbing up and down with the mom's every movement. We watched the babies grow dramatically over the course of a week. The thing that kept coming back to me, as I watched this drama every day, was how dependent the babies were on their mother. Those baby hummingbirds didn't have a prayer without Mom!

The mom kept flitting back to the nest, over and over and over. She was there to feed her babies every hour. And without that constant nurturing and feeding, those babies would have been history. It was a vivid lesson in dependence. There's no way those babies could have made it on their own. They couldn't have done it themselves. I think those babies know how much they depend on Mom, but we're not like those babies. We like to think we can do it ourselves.

By her own admission, my wife, Holly, was a stubborn little girl. When she was little and had trouble doing something, her mom and dad would offer to help. I'll bet you know the words she used in response to her parents. She would say, "I can do it myself!" She insisted on trying to do it on her own. I have in my mind this image of Holly turning on her heels and marching back to her room, defiant in her assertion that she could handle things on her own.

Diane is a woman who has multiple sclerosis. She's paralyzed. She has to be fed everything and pushed in a wheelchair. Her fingers are curled and rigid. Her voice is barely a whisper. Some people might look at her and say, "What a shame. Her life doesn't have any meaning. She can't really do anything." She *can't* do anything herself. But every morning, Diane turns her head slightly to look at the corkboard on her wall. She looks at each thumb-tacked card on her prayer list. Every torn piece of paper carefully pinned in a row. Then her lips start moving. She's praying.

She can't do anything on her own. But she knows that her prayers do big things. She moves mountains that block the paths of missionaries. She helps open the eyes of people who are spiritually blind. She prays for homeless mothers and single parents and abused children.

She can't do it herself. But she prays to a God who can. She's on the front lines, advancing the gospel of Jesus and holding up people who are hurting. We might see her as weak, but she's powerful! She's doing more than most of us who are able-bodied. And it's all because she knows she can't do it herself!

Dependence means that we start from our knees and not from our feet. Have you learned that lesson? Do you have a daily quiet time where you confess your weakness and ask for God's strength? If you don't have a designated time for prayer, let me urge you to start today. You'll be stunned to see the power that God pours into your life once you admit you can't do it yourself! Sometimes, God reduces us to weakness so that we can learn his strength.

PRAYER:

"Father, I feel the pressure of the world to advertise my strengths and camouflage my weaknesses. I resist the invitation to let others know that I have no power in and of myself to do anything. Relieve me of this pressure. Help me always to point out that I can do nothing apart from you. Teach me the ways in which you capitalize on my inadequacy. Mentor me in how to rely on you instead of relying on myself."

PRACTICAL SUGGESTIONS:

1. Offer a prayer of thanks for weaknesses in your life. I don't mean spiritual weaknesses but other dimensions of your life where God can use your weakness to exercise his strength.
2. Ask God to show you how he might use your weaknesses to exercise and reveal his strength to you and others.

DISCUSSION QUESTIONS:

1. Read 2 Corinthians 4:7–18. In what sense was Paul like a fragile clay jar? In what sense are you?
2. How did God's power transcend Paul's weakness? What was the purpose of this in Paul's life?
3. What can we learn from our powerlessness?
4. How can we learn to embrace an eternal perspective?

CHAPTER 7

The Power of Perspective

***

Now I think we are small enough.

—**Teddy Roosevelt**

I WAS ATTENDING A GRADUATE course in spiritual formation. The professors had been discussing the importance of adopting a 'rule of life,' a principle by which we would try to live going forward. They encouraged us to think of a character flaw that we wrestle with, then embrace the opposite as our rule for living (maybe something like George Costanza in *Seinfeld* determining to 'do the opposite.') Since I knew that one of my issues is sometimes pride, I shared that with the group and offered that I wanted to embrace humility as my rule of life.

I said, "Sometimes I can have the big head, can think too highly of myself." The guy sitting to my left immediately spoke up. "What could you possibly have to be proud about?" He said it in a half-joking, half-serious way. I was a little embarrassed. It stung to hear him say it. But it was a healthy reminder of the importance of being unassuming.

Maybe it's this inflated view of ourselves that sometimes causes us to inch ahead of others or to power through with others.

Most of us have a tendency to focus on ourselves. I know because I've often done that in my life. The reason I can be self-focused is not because of the way I was raised. It's not because of my temperament. It's because my ancestors were that way, and I've chosen to be just like my ancestors. My ancestors were Adam and Eve. Adam and Eve were concerned about their own glory instead of God's glory. They chose to focus on themselves instead of God. And we're the same way. We want to be the star of the show. Our name is on all the credits. We want to be the script, and we want the storyline to be all about us.

The irony is that this leaves us sad and empty. Living for yourself will starve your soul. We think, *People should love me and pay attention to me and feed my ego.* Sadly, we end up destroying ourselves. Living a me-first life is miserable. Jesus said, "What good is it for someone to gain the whole world, and yet lose or forfeit their very self?" (Luke 9:25)

FOCUS ON THE GLORY OF GOD

To find yourself, focus on the glory of God. Our problem is perspective. We think we are much bigger than we really are. We inflate ourselves and deflate God. Let me take you to Isaiah, chapter 40. In 586 BCE, the Babylonians invaded the city of Jerusalem. Think 9/11, only much worse. The Babylonians broke through the walls and poured into the city. They killed thousands of people. They captured the king of Judah. They took 70,000 people as their slaves. They hauled them off 500 miles to captivity in Babylon.

Imagine a terrorist attack on your city. The terrorists kill most of your family and friends. They drag you off to some forsaken place thousands of miles away. You've been in captivity for fifty years, and there's no end in sight. How would you feel? The people of Israel have given up on God. They think the Babylonians are bigger than God. They think, men are big, God is small. So Isaiah reminds them of the greatness of God, the glory of God. Persecuted people need to be reminded of the power of God. But proud people also need to be reminded of the power of God. God's power has a way of putting us in our place.

A BRIEF WALK THROUGH ISAIAH 40

"Who has measured the waters in the hollow of his hand, or with the breadth of his hand marked off the heavens? Who has held the dust of the earth in a basket, or weighed the mountains on the scales and the hills in a balance?" (Isaiah 40:12) Let's suppose we all went to Chicago and I gave you a one-gallon bucket. I say, "Let's form a bucket brigade and empty Lake Michigan." Lake Michigan is a hundred miles wide, 600 miles long, and 902 feet deep at its deepest point. God says, "You take all the great lakes, all the great oceans of the world, all the waters of the Earth—I can hold them in the hollow of my hand." God takes the Rockies, the Himalayas, the Andes, and weighs them on a tiny scale.

"He sits enthroned above the circle of the earth, and its people are like grasshoppers. He stretches out the heavens like a canopy, and spreads them out like a tent to live in." (Isaiah 40:22) We are microscopic compared to God. The amazing thing is that we only see the edges of what God can do. God is capable of infinitely more than we are able to see. Think about a time when you were stunned by a sunset or the miracle of a new baby. These are just fragments of what God can do. But every day, God is doing miracles right in front of us. God doesn't shock us with an occasional demonstration of deity. He displays his power every day. Every sunrise is spectacular. But we're jaded, so that we yawn over the sensational. We're in an art gallery of God's creativity, content to stare at the carpet.

"He brings princes to naught and reduces the rulers of this world to nothing. No sooner are they planted, no sooner are they sown, no sooner do they take root in the ground, than he blows on them and they wither." (Isaiah 40:23–24) Isaiah knew how feeble kings and presidents and politicians are. He had watched four kings come and go. He had seen God strike King Uzziah with leprosy because of his presumption. He knew that rulers could be literally blown away.

"To whom will you compare me? Or who is my equal? Says the Holy One. Lift your eyes and look to the heavens: Who created all these? He who brings out the starry host one by one, and calls them each by name?" (Isaiah 40. vv. 25–26) This is what God is getting at and what the prophet Isaiah is helping us see.

Teddy Roosevelt used to play a game with a friend of his. They would go out on the lawn and search the skies until they found the faint spot of light-mist beyond the lower left-hand corner of the Great Square of Pegasus. Then one of them would say, "That is the Spiral Galaxy in Andromeda. It is as large as our Milky Way. It is one of a hundred million galaxies. It consists of one billion suns, each larger than our sun." Then Roosevelt would grin and say, "Now I think we are small enough! Let's go to bed!"

We have a hard time recognizing things of greater value. But we must ascribe the most worth to what is most worthy. When our glory is more important to us than God's, we are loving ourselves more than God. We are pathetic at being God. We're not built to bear the weight of being worshipped. This is why God invites us to die to ourselves. To unself our lives. God is not honored when we focus on ourselves.

MOVING INTO REALITY

We have to move in the direction of reality instead of trying to construct a reality that will ultimately crumble. We have to reorder our loves. We have to live for the glory of God. Because God alone is great and worthy of our worship. When we put God in the highest place, the desire for our own glory is drowned out. Nothing destroys narcissism like worshipping God.

In C. S. Lewis's children's series, *The Chronicles of Narnia*, the young heroine, Lucy, meets a majestic lion named Aslan in the enchanted land of Narnia. The kids make a return visit a year later. They discover that everything has changed radically, and they quickly become lost. They go through some terrifying events. But then Lucy finally spots Aslan in a forest clearing. She rushes to him, throws her arms around his neck, and buries her face in his mane.

The great beast rolled over on his side so that Lucy fell, half sitting and half lying between his front paws. He bent forward and touched her nose with his tongue. His warm breath came all around her. She gazed up into the large wise face. "Welcome child," he said. "Aslan," said Lucy, "you're bigger." "That's because you're older, little one," answered he. "Not because you are?" "I'm not. But each year you grow, you'll find me bigger."

The more you grow in Christ, the bigger God will be. We're called to worship our way out of narcissism and self-indulgence.

Acts chapter 12 has a powerful example of what happens when you focus on yourself. King Herod thinks he is big stuff. He is all about himself. "And an appointment with Herod was granted. When the day arrived, Herod put on his royal robes, sat on his throne, and made a speech to them. The people gave him a great ovation, shouting, 'It's the voice of a god, not of a man.' Instantly, an angel of the Lord struck Herod with a sickness because he accepted the people's worship instead of giving the glory to God. So, he was consumed with worms and died." (Acts 12:21–23)

Egocentric people can't approach God. Proud people can't approach God because they have another god, self. You were not created to be the center of the universe. Our self-focused culture is nothing new. It was born in the Garden of Eden. It's been wrecking people's lives ever since. It's all about who's first, who's taking care of me, what's in it for me, there should be more for me. Augustine said the essence of sin is 'curving in on oneself.' George MacDonald said, "The one principle of hell is 'I am my own.'"

This is deadly to you and deadly to your relationships. This is especially true in marriage. Marriage only works when two people die to themselves. There will always be problems when one or both spouses refuse to die to self. When selfishness supersedes love. "What about me?" "I am first, second, and third." "I won't be overlooked." "No one will step on me." "I will not bow down to anyone." "If I'm not happy, I will leave and get a divorce." There will always be problems in a marriage when one or both partners refuse to die to self.

A mother was preparing a pancake breakfast for her little boys, Kevin and Ryan. The boys started to argue over who would get the first pancake. Their mom saw the perfect opportunity for teaching a lesson. "Now, boys, hold on a minute here. Let me tell you: If Jesus were sitting here, he would say, 'Let my brother have the first pancake. I can wait.'" The boys were silent for a moment. Then the five-year-old, Kevin, turned to his younger brother. "Okay, Ryan, you be Jesus."

That's the challenge, isn't it? Choosing to be like Jesus when the pressure is on—choosing to use our position and power not for our own advantage but for the blessing of others. This is the challenge we face in conversations. The challenge we face every time the credit card comes out. *Is my life about getting or giving?* We face it every time we're in a conflict at home or at work. *Am I going to focus only on my feelings and preferences, or is there a legitimate hurt or hunger on the other side that I could somehow serve?* We face this every time we come to worship: *Is the purpose of this to meet my preferences or to give glory to God and encourage others?*

Do you know what it is to be broken? Proud people feel smug about how much they know. Broken people realize how much they have to learn. Proud people are constantly posturing for other people. Broken people don't obsess over what other people think of them. Proud people are busy constructing an image of themselves. Broken people just want to be authentic and shed any masks.

OUR NEED FOR HUMILITY

The story is told of a Fortune 500 CEO who was driving through the countryside with his wife. They stopped for gas at a service station (this was in the days when gas stations offered real service [think *Back to the Future*]). The attendant came out to assist while the CEO went inside to pay. The attendant discovered that he knew the CEO's wife—in fact, the two had dated in high school. The CEO returned to the car, and his wife shared the information that she had dated the attendant years before. They drove on down the road. The CEO said to his wife, "I bet I know what you are thinking. I bet you are thinking, 'I'm so glad I married you, a CEO, instead of him, the service station attendant.'" His wife responded, "No, I was actually thinking that if I had married him, he would be a CEO and you would be a service station attendant." Which goes to show that greatness is a matter of perspective, huh?

If you want to gain perspective, here are some red flags to look for as you do a self-inventory.

Is the sinful nature encroaching on your life? There's no such thing as the status quo where your soul is concerned. You are either maturing in Christ or falling backward. When you tenaciously hold onto your sinful nature, you stop changing. You actually lose ground spiritually. Satan tugs you back into old sinful habits and ways of thinking.

Are you seeing things through God's eyes or your own? Your spiritual perception depends on your connection with God. When you refuse to die to yourself, you stop seeing things like God sees them. You lose contact with the heart of God. You start making excuses for sin in your life. You justify things you used to recognize as wrong. If you don't choose to take up the cross every day, you become spiritually blind. I have watched this happen to so many people. I have watched people I would have considered spiritually mature go into a downward spiral. They get so caught up in sin they don't even recognize sin in their lives. They are willing to destroy their relationship with God, their family, and all the people around them.

Are you thriving or diminishing in your spiritual vitality? If you refuse to die to yourself, you lose spiritual vitality. Your walk with God becomes a checklist to go through instead of a living relationship. You check off the boxes of going to worship and reading your Bible. But your heart is not growing in relationship to God.

To find yourself, focus on the glory of God.

QUESTION: Are you trying to get affirmation from others or from God? Whose response is more important to you?

PRAYER:

"Father, remind me of your infinite power and my infinitesimal strength. Forgive me for thinking that I am big stuff. Show me the foolishness of underestimating you and overestimating myself. Cut me down to size, dear Lord. Finish the work you began in me by transforming me into your image. Help me never to forget that you are unlimited while I am incredibly limited."

PRACTICAL SUGGESTION:

Consider the following exercise. John Ortberg identifies different kinds of me.[11] Which of these do you think you are now? Which of these would you like to be?

1. The Me I Pretend to Be. This is the kind of me promoted by the selfie culture. I pretend and pose and project an image of who I am. I'm an imposter. But I want to keep up appearances, so I pretend to be somebody I'm not.
2. The Me I Think I Should Be. We play the game of comparison. We measure ourselves against other people. Their careers or cars or houses. Or their spiritual accomplishments or spiritual gifts.
3. The Me Other People Want Me to Be. Everyone in your life wants you to change. Everybody has an agenda for you. Your boss, your coach, your family. It's easy to find yourself living to please other people.
4. The Me I'm Afraid God Wants Me to Be. A recent study by the Barna Group found that the number one challenge to helping

people grow spiritually is that most people equate spiritual maturity with trying hard to follow the rules in the Bible. Too many perceive maturity in Christ to be a matter of information, rather than transformation.

5. The Me I Am Meant to Be. God's opinion is the only one that counts. We recognize that we are people of immeasurable worth because we're made in the image of God. The Bible tells us in many places what God thinks of us. It tells us that he loves us despite our sinfulness. It tells us that we are fearfully and wonderfully made, that we are of incredible value to him. It tells us that when we turn to Christ in repentance and faith, we can be forgiven for our sins and be made new from the inside out. It tells us that in Christ, we are filled with his Spirit and destined for glory.

DISCUSSION QUESTIONS:

1. Read Isaiah 40. What are the characteristics of God that the people of Israel needed to remember?
2. Look at Isaiah 40:29. What does God promise to do for the weak?
3. Read Hebrews 11:34. How did God help his people move from weakness to strength?
4. How have you experienced the faithfulness of God in your life?

CHAPTER 8

The Power of a New Wardrobe

✳✳✳

The world breaks everyone. And afterward, some are stronger in the broken places.

—Ernest Hemingway

JOE SIMPSON IS A MOUNTAINEER who was thousands of feet up the side of the Siula Grande mountain. His safety line was cut. He had a broken leg. He slid with a broken leg into a deep crevasse. He tried several times to climb up and out of the crevasse. But since his leg was broken, he couldn't do it. So he went against his survival instinct. He made the excruciating choice to lower himself deeper into the crevasse, in the hope there would be other exits further down. The whole time he was wondering, *Am I lowering myself to freedom or just deeper into the center of the Earth? Will I see a ray of sunlight in this pit, showing me a way out? Or will I be trapped in darkness and death?* As he lowered himself down, it looked like he was moving further and further away from life. But it turned out that moving down was the only way out.

Simpson had a choice—he could try to climb up out of the crevasse, which he just couldn't do. Or he could lower himself deeper into the crevasse. Thankfully, he made the right choice. Instead of trying to elevate himself, he chose to lower himself. This is the irony of the Christian life: When you follow Christ, the way up is down.

Our culture is just the opposite: We live in a world of self-promotion, self-indulgence, and self-aggrandizement. But Jesus makes it clear that if you want to follow him, you can't be about yourself. "Whoever wants to be my disciple must deny themselves and take up their cross daily and follow me. For whoever wants to save their life will lose it, but whoever loses their life for me will save it." (Luke 9:23)

THREE DIFFERENT VERSIONS OF SELF

The Bible describes three different versions of self. First, there is the Created Self. The created self was perfect. This is the self that God created in Adam and Eve. "God saw all that he had made, and it was very good." (Genesis 1:31) Adam and Eve were completely God-focused. They had a healthy view of themselves. They knew they were significant and supremely loved. They never had any questions about their self-worth. Adam didn't feel any need to promote himself because he had already been promoted by God.

Man had been assigned a place of honor. Adam and Eve were in a state of complete innocence. They were perfect, and everything around them was perfect. Every deluxe feature that any human being might need was present on planet Earth. God formed a perfect wife from Adam's body. He told Adam and Eve to enjoy a life of lovemaking and childbearing. So, the self created by God was flawless. The created self was perfect.

Second, there is the Corrupted Self. Even though man was given great honor, he was also given one limitation. God said "You are free to eat from any tree in the garden, but you must not eat from the tree of the knowledge of good and evil, for when you eat from it you will certainly die." (Genesis 2:16–17) What was the big deal about eating the fruit? The problem was that eating the fruit represented man's desire to be like God.

But Satan countered with the rebuttal that eating the fruit would not result in death. Remember, Satan is a liar and the father of lies. So in the moment when Adam and Eve thumbed their noses at God, the sinful self was born. The sinful self is the seed of Satan, the direct result of man trying to be God instead of man obeying God. Sin corrupted our DNA. Instead of man living for God, man decided to live for himself.

This focus on self is found in the words of shock rocker Alice Cooper: "Ain't gonna spend my life being no one's fool. I was born to rock and I was born to rule... I never learned to bow, bend, or crawl to any known authority. I really want to build my statue tall... I just wanna be God." (In a dramatic shift in his life. more recently Cooper has expressed faith in Christ and a desire to dedicate his life to God). Deep inside, this is what we all want—to be our own god.

Adam and Eve had been given an entire planet. But that wasn't enough. They weren't content to have dominion over the Earth. They wanted to have dominion over everything. In other words, they wanted to be God. The most immediate death they experienced wasn't physical. It was spiritual. This ruptured their relationship with God. Not only that, but sin contaminated our whole planet.

So the corrupted self wants to dominate your life. The corrupted self demands that your life be all about you. You were born thinking the world revolves around you. That the universe exists to make you happy. You were born to believe in the me-first philosophy. The mantra of the corrupted culture is, it's all about you. It's all about self. The corrupted self was poisoned.

Third, there is the Recreated Self. This is the self that God wants to restore. He wants to take you back to the Garden of Eden and give you the life that Adam and Eve enjoyed. But he knows you can't do this on your own. He knew that Adam's sin poisoned all of humanity. He knew that it would take a new Adam, a different human being, to restore his original design. That's why he sent Christ to be the new Adam. The created self was perfect. The corrupted self came through Adam. Adam grasped for godlike status and plunged the world into sin and death. Jesus humbled himself, was plunged into a shameful death so we could have our glory restored.

When Christ comes to live inside us, we experience the recreated self. We celebrate a full and abundant life. This is a precursor to the fruition of our life in eternity. Imagine yourself as you are but free from the negative drag of the Fall. The new you in eternity. The person God intended you to be. Who you are without all the flaws and dysfunctions and imperfections of this life. You're redeemed to live into the reality of your new self—your positives amplified and your personality fully matured.

DYING TO SELF

But how do we find our way back to the recreated self? How do we rediscover our true element? It starts with the cross. It's something only God can do. The only thing we contribute to our salvation is the sin that makes it necessary. But the Bible is clear that Christ is not the only one to go to the cross.

"For you died, and your life is now hidden with Christ in God." (Colossians. 3:3) Paul says that you died with Christ. The end of you is where real life begins. This means saying no to the world and yes to God. This means choosing the cross every day. This means dying to yourself. I've noticed something about dead people. They don't seem to care much about what other people think of them. They're not concerned about polishing their image. Not concerned about fancy clothes or the stock market or promotions. Paul says you died. Now you have new life in Christ. Our problem is that we want the resurrection without the grave. We want new life without dying to ourselves.

"For we know that our old self was crucified with him so that the body ruled by sin might be done away with, that we should no longer be slaves to sin." (Romans 6:6) In other words, there was a definitive break with sin. The old man stands in stark contrast with the new man. Salvation is transformation. It isn't adding a new self to the old self. The old self doesn't exist anymore.

But ditching the old and putting on the new is a continuous process.

"You were taught, with regard to your former way of life, to put off your old self, which is being corrupted by its deceitful desires; to be made new in the attitude of your minds; and to put on the new self, created to be like God in true righteousness and holiness." (Ephesians 4:22–24) Following Christ is a radical change, a conversion. It means repudiating your old self. Your old self was corrupt and falling apart. The verb 'corrupt' means to ruin or destroy something. Self was disintegrating. Dominated by deceitful desires. But you were taught to take off the old self and scrap it for good.

You were also taught to put on the new self. "Created to be like God in true righteousness and holiness." This is God's creative activity. In other words, this is your recreated self. This is God's original design for you. You experienced a brand-new creation. "Therefore, if anyone is in Christ, the new creation has come: The old has gone, the new is here." (2 Corinthians 5:17) The image of God was lost in Adam. But when Christ becomes your life, the image of God is restored.

Dying to self is a ruthless experience. Dietrich Bonhoeffer wrote: "When Christ calls a man, he bids him come and die." C.S. Lewis put it bluntly: "Christ says 'Give me All. I don't want so much of your time and so much of your money and so much of your work: I want you. I have not come to torment your natural self, but to kill it.'"

If this sounds severe, it is. But as always, God's demands flow from his mercy and his unrelenting desire to give us freedom and genuine life. He doesn't want us to settle for less than the very best. Listen again to Lewis:

> I don't want to cut off a branch here and a branch there, I want to have the whole tree down... *Hand over the whole natural self, all the desires which you think innocent as well as the ones you think wicked—the whole outfit. I will give you a new self instead. In fact, I will give you Myself: my own will shall become yours.*

A NOTE FROM MY WIFE

Right after Holly and I got married, I came home to find a note attached to some of the clothes in my closet. The note said, *These go.* This was Holly's not-so-subtle way of telling me to scrap some part of my wardrobe. These were clothes in my closet I was proud of. Knit suits. Sansa belt slacks. Bell-bottom trousers. But Holly made it clear—these things had to go.

This is what Paul is telling us. You were taught to put off your old self. This happened when you were baptized. "So in Christ Jesus you are all children of God through faith, for all of you who were baptized into Christ have clothed yourselves with Christ." (Galatians 3:26–27) In other words, you threw out the old wardrobe and put on a brand-new set of clothes. Clothes make the man. So learn how to dress for success. Put off the old and put on the new.

If you go to a rescue mission, you sometimes see a delousing room, where street people who haven't had a bath in months discard their old clothes. The old clothes are burned, and new clothes are handed out. This is what happens when you're saved. Except that you're not just given a bath, you're given a brand-new nature.

A friend of mine ran an inner-city ministry for years. One Sunday, he noticed a woman wearing a red dress and high heels, sitting in the back row for worship. As my friend looked more closely, he recognized that the woman was actually a man—a frequent attender of church each week. The man enjoyed wearing women's clothing as a fetish but had never revealed this sin to anyone before.

My friend confronted the man about his wrong behavior. Together, they went to the man's house, where he removed the dress and instead put on men's clothes. Then they returned to worship with the church, where the red dress was put in a barrel and burned in front of the whole faith community. It was a graphic way of saying goodbye to the old wardrobe of sin.

A NEW WARDROBE

So, it isn't enough to put on the new clothes just one time. You have to live in a way that's consistent with your new wardrobe. It's popular to buy athletic clothing these days. It's called athleisure, sold by Nike and other popular brands. The market for athleisure may hit $100 billion this year. But here's the weird thing. Most people are just wearing it, not actually working out in it. The *New York Times* says, "The athletic part of athleisure is aspirational. [For example], sales of yoga clothes increased 10 times as much as [actual] participation in yoga classes over the 2009 to 2014 span." In other words, we like the workout look; we just don't like the workout lifestyle or the workout practices.

What are some signs that you haven't put off the old self? Name-dropping. Mirror-looking. Calling attention to yourself. Putting other people down. Choosing friends based on what they'll do for your image. Talking over the top of other people. Always having to get your way. Needing to win every argument. Grabbing credit whenever you can. Never being able to apologize. Leaving God out of the conversation. Thinking that it's always about you. I thought about titling this chapter, "You're so vain, you probably think this chapter is about you."

Pride pushes God off the podium. God becomes an afterthought. We might not think about God at all. We put ourselves ahead of others. But how do we learn to be broken of ourselves? How do we take off the old self and put on the new self? Brokenness requires both God's initiative and our response.

Dying to self is not a feeling or an emotion. It's a partnership between you and the Holy Spirit. You choose to take off the old self and put on the new, asking the Spirit to sustain you as you jettison the old self. It's a constant way of life. It's being shattered of your self-will. Brokenness is a lifestyle. It's saying yes when God calls and no whenever the world calls. "My sacrifice, O God, is a broken spirit; a broken and contrite heart you, God, will not despise." (Psalm 51:16)

You may be thinking, *There's no way I can do that.* Or maybe you find yourself negotiating with God: "I'll go to anyone but not that person... I'll do anything but not that one thing..." But if you want to experience the blessings of brokenness, you have to choose to run head-on into whatever it is that your pride is telling you not to do.

It's easy to live with the philosophy—believe in yourself. But the purpose of your life is not to get glory for yourself. The purpose of your life is to give glory to God. "It's in Christ that we find out who we are and what we are living for. Long before we first heard of Christ and got our hopes up, he had his eye on us, had designs on us for glorious living, part of the overall purpose he is working out in everything and everyone." (Ephesians 1:11–12) We're not here to live for the praise of our glory—we're here to live for the praise of his glory. And the surprising reward for pursuing the glory of God is that as we do, we experience the serendipity of discovering our true selves for the first time.

PRAYER:

"Father, please give me a new wardrobe. Help me exchange the old clothes of selfishness for new clothes of serving and giving. Show me how the tattered and dingy threads of sin interfere with my joy and your ability to use me. Help me to be willing to strip off the ugly gear of sin and self and exchange that gear for the new clothes of righteousness."

PRACTICAL SUGGESTIONS:

There are at least three things God uses to bring us to a point of brokenness.

1. Stay glued to the Word of God. The Word has the power to help you dump the old self and take on the new. God says, "Is not my word... like a hammer that breaks the rock in pieces?"

(Jeremiah 23:29) "For the word of God is alive and powerful. It is sharper than the sharpest two-edged sword, cutting between soul and spirit, between joint and marrow. It exposes our innermost thoughts and desires." (Hebrews 4:12) Nothing breaks my selfishness like the Word of God. You don't just read the Bible—it reads you. The Bible has the power to penetrate your defenses and expose your spiritual blind spots. If you want to put on the new self, you have to stay in the Word.

2. Recognize God's ability to redeem and recreate you through circumstances. God sometimes uses circumstances to break us. He uses circumstances to help us throw off the old self and put on the new. I don't mean that all the circumstances in your life are orchestrated by God. But I do mean that God often allows you to go through certain circumstances so that he can soften your heart. It could be a financial crisis or a tough situation at work or some other personal challenge that he leverages for your growth and maturity.

Jennifer Kennedy Dean encourages us to see the difficult circumstances of our lives as 'crucifixion moments':

Every time you are confronted with a crucifixion moment, choose to lay down your self-life. Choose to surrender your pride, your expectations, your rights, your demands. Choose the way of the cross. Let someone else get the credit you deserve; forego the opportunity to have the last word; die to the demands of your flesh.[12]

3. Choose to be broken—don't wait for God to break you. "Humble yourself under the mighty hand of God." (1 Peter 5:6) "Humble yourselves before the Lord, and he will lift you up." (James 4:10) The fact is, everybody's going to be broken—sooner or later. We can choose to be broken, or we can wait for God to crush our

pride. You can spare yourself a ton of pain and heartache if you choose to let God break you now.

DISCUSSION QUESTIONS:

1. Have you ever had the blessing of a new wardrobe? How did it make you feel?
2. Read Ephesians 4:20–32. What are some things in your life you need to 'take off'? To 'put on'?
3. Read Ephesians 1:12–14. What is our purpose in life? How can we fulfill that purpose?
4. Read Galatians 6:1–3. What do we need to learn from each other?

CHAPTER 9

The Power of Identity

✳✳✳

Because even though I have become somebody, I still have to prove that I am somebody. My struggle has never ended and I guess it never will.

—Madonna

THE CRUCIAL ISSUE: OUR IDENTITY

HOW WOULD YOU IDENTIFY YOURSELF? If I asked who you are, what would you say? Some of you would talk about your family, the number of kids in your family, etc. Some of you would talk about what you do for a living. If you're a student, you might say you're involved in sports or debate or band or cheerleading. Or you might talk about your achievements. "I went to state in wrestling." "I graduated in the top 10 percent of my class." "I have tons of followers on Instagram." "I once ate two dozen Krispy Kremes in one sitting." (If you accomplished this gastronomical success, you may want to consider challenging Joey Chesnutt next July in the Nathan's hot dog contest).

Your identity is the linchpin of your spiritual and emotional health. If you are looking for inner peace, it starts with a healthy identity. But how do we find our identity when there's so much pressure to keep reinventing ourselves? Avatars are so popular in our culture that some spend time on social media developing false identities instead of living out their real identities. The crucial question is this: How do we find an environment where we can develop a healthy identity?

A SQUIRREL IN OUR TOILET

About a year after Holly and I got married, I went one morning into the bathroom. I was about to take a shower but first lifted the toilet lid. Out leaped a wet, fuzzy creature bouncing all over our bathroom and then taking a flying jump into our tub. I didn't know what it was, but it was screeching at the top of its voice. I quickly shut the bathroom door as I exited the bathroom and announced to Holly, "Whatever you do, do not go into the bathroom."

I hustled to the garage and found a hammer and a pair of gloves. I'm not sure what I thought I would do, armed with my fighting equipment, but I was prepared to do battle. I went back to the bathroom door, boldly marching in. No, the truth is, I hesitantly peered into the room, and there it was—a squirrel in our bathtub, still going nuts and screaming.

I called the city animal control unit and explained that we had a squirrel in our bathroom. When the truck arrived, the worker walked in with a long rod with a small noose on the end. After considerable effort, he was able to slip the noose around the squirrel's neck and remove the varmint from our house. We were ever so glad!

I was still puzzled about how the squirrel had found entry into our bathroom. As it turned out, we had had some plumbing issues, and I had turned off the water pressure the night before at the base of the commode. The squirrel had slinked down a pipe on the top of our house and crept into the toilet, where it had spent the night. Once the lid was lifted, it lurched into the tub!

I told this story to the church the next Sunday—I think there were people who didn't go to the bathroom for a few days! At our next fellowship lunch, one of our members brought a dish that he insisted I try—it was fried squirrel (I'm not making this up). It was actually not bad—tasted a bit like chicken!

A few weeks later, I traveled to California and stayed with Holly's parents for a few days. After unloading my suitcase, I went into the bathroom and lifted the lid. I was greeted by a ceramic rabbit, which my mother-in-law had placed in the toilet as a joke. It was hilarious—but I was thankful it didn't come flying out of the commode!

HUMAN BEINGS HAVE AN ELEMENT

It is a goofy story, but I think this communicates an important truth. I've thought about why the squirrel was so frightened. I believe it's because he was trapped in an environment in which he was never designed to live. He was out of his element. His intended element is outdoors, where he can scamper and play and search for food. The reason he was so undone is because he was in a totally alien environment.

For any of us to flourish, we have to live in the element God originally intended. Squirrels have an element as do human beings. The only healthy element for a human being is in the grace and will of God. Whenever we forget the grace of God, we find ourselves confused and uncertain. Anytime we try to find our value through others instead of God, we're destined to be intimidated, lost, and terribly frightened.

Unfortunately, we're tempted to live outside of the element God designed for us. We're tempted to live in the world of performance. The world of comparison. We find ourselves scrambling and screeching and our nerves frazzled. We will never really find ourselves as long as we are separated from our true element.

ZOOCHOSIS

To use another illustration, think about zoo exhibits that have been created for lions. These environments have been designed by experts who have spent lifetimes studying lions and their habitats. The exhibits are intended to simulate as closely as possible the natural habitat of the lion. But no matter how successful the experts may be, the reality is that the lion keeps pacing. Instinctively, he knows that this is not the element in which he was designed to live. Not only does the lion know it, but we know it too.

There is a term for this. Zoochosis is the common term for what lions do at the zoo when they pace back and forth in their cages. These are animals driven to psychosis from being in captivity.

The sad reality is that we human beings suffer from a similar psychosis. We're living in an environment never designed for us. We're pacing back and forth because we find ourselves in an alien setting. We're living in a culture that pushes us to compete and perform. This can be suffocating, cutting us off from the oxygen of God and his grace. Instead of living in the wide-open spaces of God's grace, we're confined to cages that deprive us of the freedom God wants us to experience. We are desperate to assert ourselves. Frantic to find ourselves. Maybe we are like the caged lion who has spent its entire life locked up—we have been in captivity so long that we don't even know what genuine freedom is all about.

THE SELF-HELP MOVEMENT

A factor nudging us to compete and compare is the self-help movement. An article in *New Yorker* magazine reports that the self-help movement has mushroomed into an $11-billion-dollar industry. Bookstore shelves overflow with advice on everything imaginable. One book is entitled *How to Make People Like You in 90 Seconds or Less*. With the help of this book, you can learn how to make a lasting good impression, from teeth to breath to handshake to small talk. Another volume is titled *59 Seconds: Change Your Life in Under a Minute*. This book promises behavioral tweaks in any amount of time anyone can spare.

The self-help movement promotes the idea that we can save ourselves and overcome our problems through our own efforts. That we have the ability to help ourselves out of all of our problems, no matter how sticky or challenging. But the chaos that characterizes our society stems directly from the misconception that our identities are grounded in self.

I CAN'T HELP MYSELF

Of course, God wants us to know that we are people of worth. He wants us to have a strong view of self. But our culture paradoxically pushes us in the direction of not finding ourselves and instead damaging ourselves. *It is the ultimate irony: In seeking to find ourselves, we end up losing a sense of who we really are.*

We're desperate to discover ourselves. We're about self-help, self-esteem, self-discovery, self-fulfillment, and self-improvement. It's fun and insightful to learn about my temperament and my personality. But the problem is, self is the wrong starting point. *I can never really know who I am until I know the God who made me who I am.*

A.W. Tozer wrote, "What comes into our minds when we think about God is the most important thing about us." God defines you. You can't find yourself without first finding God. When you discover who God is, you discover who you are. When you discover who you are, you don't have to struggle with insecurity and promoting yourself. The irony is that you can find yourself by forgetting yourself.

Narcissus was a character in Greek mythology, well known for his looks and vanity. One day, he stopped at a pool to drink. He was mesmerized by his reflection. He was so obsessed with his image that he died beside the pool. Someone captured the pitfall of his self-absorption in a limerick:

> There once was a nymph named Narcissus, who thought himself very delicious;
> So he stared like a fool, at his face in a pool, and his folly today is still with us.

THREE OPTIONS IN THINKING OF YOURSELF

In his first letter to the Corinthians, Paul describes the challenge of defending his ministry. His critics in Corinth argued, "Paul is a nobody. He's not a polished speaker. He doesn't have a commanding physical presence." They were comparing Paul with other leaders. His detractors were discrediting him and judging him, bragging about themselves and putting him down.

So Paul faced a personal dilemma. How would he respond to his critics? He might have been tempted to spend time outperforming others. Or distributing a resume that made him look good. He knew what it was to be discredited. Tim Keller points out that Paul has three options to consider.[13]

Option one: Paul could choose to promote himself. He could respond by rushing to his own defense. By boasting of his achievements and credentials. He could get online and post ancient equivalents to selfies for the Corinthians to read. But Paul refuses to boast. Paul knows that bragging is a source of division and strife. He won't go there. His message in 1 Corinthians 3:21 is: "I don't want to hear you bragging about yourself or anyone else."

But we often resist this option. We feel compelled to perform. To achieve. We want to be somebody, to prove that we count. We want other people's stamp of approval. Madonna was interviewed by *Vogue* magazine. She said:

My drive in life comes from a fear of being mediocre. That is always pushing me. I push past one spell of it and discover myself as a special human being but then I feel I am still mediocre and uninteresting unless I do something else. Because even though I have become somebody, I still have to prove that I am somebody. My struggle has never ended and I guess it never will.

Option two: Paul rejects the first option, but he has another. He could choose to put himself down. He could choose to wilt in the face of his critics. He could say, "You guys are right. I'm no good. I'm a nobody. I quit. God can't use me. I might as well give up." But Paul refuses to beat himself up. To wallow in a pit of low self-esteem. Paul knows that

God sees him as a person of infinite worth. That God won't discredit him.

It's easy to sink into low self-esteem, isn't it? Because all of us fail. We can always find somebody who is more beautiful than we are or more handsome than we are. We can always find somebody who is smarter or more successful than we are. Even if we're smart or successful or beautiful, all of that is going to fade. We lose our looks and we lose our smarts and success wears off.

Option three: Paul could choose not to think about himself at all. In 1 Corinthians 4:3, Paul essentially says, "It matters very little to me what you think of me, even less where I rank in popular opinion. I don't even rank myself." Paul lives for an audience of one. What his critics think doesn't matter. The only one whose opinion matters is God. God is the one whose judgment counts.

GENUINE HUMILITY

Paul doesn't have a high view of himself. He doesn't have a low view of himself. He just doesn't think of himself much at all. Paul isn't full of himself. He isn't down on himself. He just doesn't spend time thinking about himself. He is self-forgetful. When people are down, sometimes we say, "You just need a stronger sense of self-esteem. You need to get out there and strut your stuff." But Paul is very different. His perspective is, "I don't think of myself at all. I don't look to anybody else for my sense of identity. I don't have to prove to the Corinthians that I am somebody." He doesn't get his sense of identity from them. Neither does he get it from himself. Paul's secure identity comes from his hard-wired connection with Christ.

C.S. Lewis makes a brilliant observation about what it really means to be humble.

If we were to meet a truly humble person we would never come away from meeting them thinking they were humble. They would not be always telling us they were a nobody (because a person who keeps saying they are a nobody is actually a self-obsessed person). The thing we would remember from meeting a truly gospel-humble person is how much they seemed to be totally interested in us. Because the essence of gospel-humility is not thinking more of myself or thinking less of myself, it is thinking of myself less.[14]

HUGH JACKMAN

Actor Hugh Jackman describes some of the deep wounds that still drive his life years after his childhood. When he was eight years old, his mother abandoned him, his father, and Hugh's four elder siblings. When he finally realized that his mother was gone for good, Jackman was too frightened to enter his house alone. "I was terrified because I was the first one home every day. I used to walk home from school and wait outside. I just wouldn't go in." His father, Christopher, seemed to compensate for the pain by working long hours as an accountant. Jackman said, "My father could only come to one game a year because he had five kids, and on Saturday he had to shop. If my father was there, it would be 50 percent greater. Having his approval is something that still drives me."

Jackman admits his ongoing struggles with fear, anxiety, and people-pleasing. He's still driven to be somebody. "I saw a play in Sydney, and in the notes they had this quote from Bono that said: 'What kind of hole exists in the heart of a person when they need to have 70,000 people scream, "I love you," in order to feel fulfilled?' But there is a part of me that wants to please, to be all things to all people."[15]

This dynamic of wanting to be *somebody* is what drives much of our passion to prove our value. But faith says that you are someone of unlimited value—not because of what you do or how you look but because of what Christ has done. You're significant—not because you have outperformed other people but because you put your trust in the performance of Christ.

Paul reminds us that our position before God isn't predicated on our achievements but the achievement of God through Christ: his message in Romans 4:4–5 is: "If you're a hard worker and do a good job, you deserve your pay; we don't call your wages a gift. But if you see that the job is too big for you, that it's something only *God* can do, and you trust him to do it—you could never do it for yourself no matter how hard and long you worked—well, that trusting-him-to-do-it is what gets you set right with God, *by* God. Sheer gift."

PRAYER:

"Father, I am so insecure when I look to myself for validation. I feel the tug of the world to assert who I am by promoting myself instead of promoting you. Teach me that my identity is safe only when I am defined by my relationship with you. Help me surrender once and for all my tendency to see my identity as something apart from you."

PRACTICAL SUGGESTIONS:

1. Think of the three options you have in thinking about yourself. Ask God to move you to the healthiest of the three.
2. Look for a specific way you can 'promote God' this week. Find someone to serve, someone to pray for, someone to share your faith with. Then get into action!

DISCUSSION QUESTIONS:

1. How would you identify yourself? Who are you? What influences have been formative in developing your view of yourself?
2. This chapter tells the story of a squirrel that spent the night in our commode. What is the appropriate element for a squirrel? What is the appropriate element for a human being? What happens when we live outside of our element?

3. How does the self-help movement interfere with our attempts to know who we are?

4. Read 1 Corinthians 4:3. What situation is Paul dealing with? What are the three options Paul has in responding to his situation? Read Galatians 2:20. How can we move from a horizontal self to a vertical self?

CHAPTER 10

The Negative Power of Social Media

***

No one's knocking on my Facebook account door... to have to get past my brother to get to me—it's just me. And so, what ends up happening is that the actual infrastructure of the social media shapes our imaginations about where we are located in society. It shapes how we imagine ourselves to be at the center of the networks.

—Felicia Wu Song

THE USE OF SOCIAL MEDIA fuels remarkable creativity. During a National Signing Day for college football recruits, athletes adopted creative ways to call attention to themselves. One guy jumped out of an airplane with a buddy to announce his choice. Another guy did a Thriller-style video where he played the role of Michael Jackson. Another put on a Nebraska cap at the end to reveal his choice. Levi Jones from Texas sat at the podium and took off a black jumper to reveal Gators. Then Seminoles. Then Trojans—Southern Cal. Today, it's not enough to announce where you're going to school—you need to do it with selfies and lots of drama.

Social media and selfies can be fun ways to let other people know about your life. My wife and I have a selfie stick or two (even one that is attached to a tripod for better angles), and we enjoy snapping photos and sending them to our family and friends. But where is the social media culture taking us?

Often, the use of social media is in direct conflict with the power of weakness. I'm not suggesting this is inevitable, as some people leverage the power of such media for positive ends. But the nature of social media often stands in stark contrast to the power of weakness. I believe there are three areas where social media is at odds with the power of weakness.

First, a biblical view of weakness promotes a spirit of humility while the use of social media tends to move us in the direction of pride.
The power of weakness guards us against thinking too highly of ourselves. But the platforms of social media entice us to have an inordinate view of ourselves. And to project that view to others.

I recently watched the Netflix documentary *The Social Dilemma*. Experts from Silicon Valley pointed to the narcotic-like effect social media has on the brain. There's compelling evidence that getting a like or a comment can be intoxicating because of the boost of dopamine that comes from being acknowledged. This urges us to rush to social media looking for a little ego gratification.

Think about the ways in which social media encourages us to turn in on ourselves. The slogan of YouTube is 'Broadcast Yourself.' The name Facebook is just right—get your face out there, hopefully looking as good as possible. As early as 2006, *Time* magazine officially made You their Person of the Year. Time recognized that Americans have become obsessed with promoting themselves. The cover came complete with a mirror, so you could extend your self-fascination.

Extensive studies have shown that the use of social media can lead to narcissism. Consider the impact of social media on personality characteristics. Specifically, look at the effects of two popular social platforms, Facebook and X (previously known as Twitter).

Facebook: The Social Mirror (where we post images of ourselves):

- People who use Facebook the most tend to have more narcissistic or insecure personalities.

- Those with higher narcissism scores were frequently updating statuses, posting pictures of themselves, and using quotes or mottos to glorify themselves.
  *Based on a study of Facebook users ages 18–25 using the Narcissism Personality Inventory and Rosenberg Self-Esteem Scale

X: The Social Megaphone (where we post messages about ourselves):

- In a University of Michigan study of college undergraduates, it was found that those who scored higher in narcissism also posted more often on X.
- Young people are using X to broaden social circles and broadcast views. This usage leads people to overrate the importance of their opinions. (See Appendices A and B)

Another sign of the connection between social media and narcissism is the humblebrag, often seen on X. Humblebrag is practicing the art of false modesty. For instance, a businessman posts this: *Just filed my taxes. They were right, mo' money mo' problems.* Or a young lady produces this status update: *I hate when I go into a store to get something to eat and the male staff are too busy hitting on me to get my order right: (so annoying.)* Or a mother creatively praises her own parenting: *My perfect little princess brought me breakfast in bed again. So much for watching what I eat today. Oh well.* We can use social media to create a picture-perfect version of ourselves or our kids or our vacations or our lives in general. This is a not-so-subtle way of calling attention to ourselves.

Jean Twenge wrote *The Narcissism Epidemic: Living in the Age of Entitlement,* reporting on her extensive studies on the growth of narcissism in America.[16]

We didn't have to look very hard to find it. It was everywhere. On a reality TV show, a girl planning her sixteenth birthday party wants a major road blocked off so a marching band can precede her grand entrance on a red carpet. A book called My Beautiful Mommy explains plastic surgery to young children whose mothers are going under the knife for the trendy "Mommy Makeover." People strive to create a "personal brand" (also called "self-branding"), packaging themselves like a product to be sold.

The power of weakness mitigates pride while the use of social media may call us toward egotism.

Second, a biblical view of weakness urges us to be cautious about seeking the spotlight while the use of social media tends to move us in the direction of notoriety.

The power of weakness helps us be content to serve behind the scenes. But social media nudges us to covet being on stage. The power of weakness enables us to be content with obscurity. Social media beckons us to thirst to be seen and known.

John Starke writes about our insatiable desire to be known and applauded.

> ...Our modern world has internalized the idea that the markers of having an admirable and successful life are primarily visible. It leads us to believe that a sense of self-worth and identity are metrics to be displayed. The performance of the self has become more important than the reality. We live as if the most important things about us are to be performed before others; that our deepest happiness will come from being who others think we ought to be." [17]

I think Jesus would be uncomfortable with our tendency to advertise ourselves through social media.

The power of weakness also summons us to share our challenges as well as our triumphs. This is not a call to publicize all of our failures. But it is a call to be honest about the fact that we don't win every game or take home every trophy. We may even have a contempt for vulnerability because we prize our autonomy and self-sufficiency.

QUESTION: Do you spend more time developing your public life or your private life? Which is more important to you: enhancing your public image or growing in your walk with Christ?

Weakness is usually the last thing we want to reveal to others. We want to project an image of ourselves as having it all together and achieving success. We're eager to let the world know that we matter—so why would we even think of disclosing our struggles? Imagine a blog that consistently reported bad grades, demotions at work, athletic failures, and career catastrophes. No one wants to parade their weaknesses—everyone wants to publicize their accomplishments.

We all have failures in our careers. We usually keep quiet about it. But a Princeton professor chose to share his list of failures on Twitter (now X) for the world to see. Professor of Psychology and Public Affairs Johannes Haushofer says that projecting nothing, but success is damaging. So he decided to do something about it. His tweet mentions "Degree programs I did not get into," "Research funding I did not get," and "Paper rejections from academic journals." Why did he do it? "Most of what I try fails, but these failures are often invisible, while the successes are visible. I have noticed that this sometimes gives others the impression that most things work out for me." [18]

Maybe we need to fast from the use of social media so we can learn the value of obscurity over notoriety.

Third, a biblical view of weakness gives us a strong sense of personal

identity while the use of social media tends to create confusion about who we are.

The power of weakness encourages a healthy and accurate view of our identity. Conversely, the use of social media tugs us almost inevitably into a distorted view of who we are.

The paradox is that while exercising social media to communicate ourselves, we sometimes lose ourselves. I wonder if we have reached a point where we have mastered the selfie but not the self? And is it possible that in our desperate attempt to advance ourselves through social media, the use of these platforms actually *interferes* with our ability to know ourselves? Are we being medi-a-ted?

Social media channels can be great tools, but we have to be careful how we use them. I borrowed my friend's chain saw and it was useful, but it didn't take me long to figure out that misusing it could be disastrous. The misuse of social media may handicap our ability to find our way back to ourselves.

LIKE CHASING

"This generation is all about branding themselves and their ideas—well before they've had a variety of experiences and relationships and the time to get comfortable in their own skin and really shore up a sense of self," says Dr. Lauren Hazzouri, a clinical psychologist. "This dilemma, what I refer to as the cart before the horse quandary, puts millennials at risk of ultimately being vulnerable to the appraisal of others, leading to what I call 'Like Chasing,' the never-ending altering and morphing. They're becoming not first-rate versions of themselves but second-rate versions of established brands (this includes personal brands such as celebrities) that people 'like' a million-plus times a day."

Mark Sayers points out that there are two ways of looking at self: the Vertical Self and the Horizontal Self. The vertical self is defined in terms of your relationship with God. The horizontal self is defined only in terms of your relationship with others.

Whereas the vertical self looks to heaven for favor and approval, the horizontal self looks to the world for approval and acceptance. For people who hold a horizontal sense of self, the creation and cultivation of a public image are paramount. Peers and society act as a mirror: we look to them to gain a sense of identity, yet they can only relay back to us the messages that we communicate to them. You cannot describe yourself as cool. Others must label you cool. In that way our identities are dependent on what others think of us. [19]

A DIVIDED MICHAEL JACKSON

Sayers gives an example of someone who seemed to struggle outside the element of God's grace and love. Many believe Michael Jackson was the world's greatest performer. A recent Broadway musical celebrates his unmistakable gifts. But some believe Jackson really transitioned from one self to another to another.

> A classic case of the fragmentation of self can be found in the media coverage of Michael Jackson's life and death. In remembering his life, the media referred to different Michael Jacksons. There was the super talented young boy of the Jackson 5; there was the young adult Michael Jackson of the Off the Wall and Thriller albums; there was the eccentric but lovable Michael Jackson of the early days of the Neverland ranch period. But then there was the seemingly darker and apparently more disturbed Michael Jackson who went on trial and who dangled his baby off a balcony. And there was the reclusive Michael Jackson of the last few years of his life. People who knew Michael Jackson would talk about "the Michael Jackson I knew" alluding to the fact that there seemed to be different Michael Jacksons.
>
> When Jackson died, some of my friends told me that they were mourning the Jackson 5 boy Michael Jackson or the Thriller

Michael Jackson but not the later Michael Jackson. All the while, everyone seemed to forget that they were discussing one man, not many. This phenomenon illuminates the way our media culture seems to split us into different selves. *The Internet has only furthered this breakdown between our real selves and our acting selves. We have now mastered the art of adapting to multiple self-images depending on our circumstances.*

I know that's an extreme case. But it's enticing to keep creating new images of ourselves to validate who we are in the eyes of others. We wake up every day to a culture that exerts enormous pressure to perform. Massive pressure to compare ourselves to others. We're surrounded by a dark hole that makes us want to compete and compare.

COMPARISONITIS

Envy may be more prevalent than ever before thanks to social media. Now, we can not only compare ourselves to those we know but to people all over the globe. This triggers a tendency to constantly compare ourselves with others, even the most glamorous and successful. One therapist has coined this as 'comparisonitis,' an *emotional* sickness. The challenge is that we are deluged with photoshopped lives. We're busy finding the perfect camera angle. We may look dazzling on the outside, but we may find ourselves empty on the inside.

Time magazine reported alarming statistics about the impact of multiple social media platforms.[20] The platforms, according to recent studies, foster a 'compare and despair' attitude. The data indicate that Instagram in particular has a negative impact on anxiety. People feel lonely, not good enough, as if they need to perform, and yet they are obsessed with the idea of being and staying liked.

One of the most insightful works regarding the connection between social media and identity is *You Are Not Your Own* by Alan Noble. He identifies two groups of people: the Affirming and the Resigned. Affirming people are driven to improve themselves. They are looking for ways to make themselves look good in the eyes of others. They want to prove that they are valuable to themselves and other people.

Then there are the Resigned. These people have accepted that they will never be able to compete with the Affirming. They have concluded that they will never be able to live up to the level of the Affirming, so they sink into despair. They dive into trivial forms of entertainment or other activities that enable them to kill time.

But whether a person belongs to the Affirming or the Resigned, there's a tendency to self-medicate. Noble writes:

> ...some binge watch Friends... some scroll endlessly through Instagram, some post endlessly on Twitter, some argue online, some obsess about their health, some obsess about the environment, some protest online, some protest to be famous online, some travel, some attempt suicide, some attempt self-improvement, some abuse people, some join extremist movements...

The truth is that we are not our own. We belong to Christ. We aren't slaves to the taskmaster of the Affirming—we have no need to prove ourselves to others or to accomplish anything to demonstrate our self-worth. Instead, we recognize that since we belong to Christ, our identity is firmly anchored in his call on our lives, nothing else. This same principle applies to the Resigned. Rather than surrendering to despair because of our inability to compete with others, we accept the invitation of Christ to do for him whatever he asks.

Listen again to Noble. Think about this: The basic story we tell ourselves in the modern world is of self-discovery. Our films, novels, and TV shows repeatedly follow the story of a protagonist who longs to know who they truly are, to uncover their authentic self, to throw off the expectations of fathers, teachers, and the rest of society in order to follow their own path.

We might even say that self-discovery is our contemporary hero's journey. Who are you? What is your personality? What motivates you? What are you passionate about? How do you perceive yourself? How do you want the world to see you? These questions are not easily answered, and our answers often change during different seasons of our lives. But what doesn't change is the obligation to answer them, to define who we are—publicly. When that obligation feels overwhelming, we call it an identity crisis. Many people suffer from a chronic identity crisis, shifting from one identity to another throughout their life."[21]

One of the most helpful tools in discovering our true selves is the power of weakness. This power guards us against thinking too highly of ourselves or too little of ourselves. This power reminds us that we are completely reliant on God for everything we are and have and do. But it also reminds us that God has made us a 'little lower than the angels' and regards us as invaluable.

I came across a fascinating verse in my study of Ephesians. Paul writes in Ephesians 1:19, "I pray that your hearts will be flooded with light so that you can understand the confident hope he has given to those he called—his holy people who are his rich and glorious inheritance."

Look at that last phrase again—'...his holy people who are his rich and glorious inheritance.' We usually think of the inheritance we will *receive* from God, and it's true that God promises a rich inheritance to those who believe in Christ. But this verse says that we also *constitute* an inheritance. We *are* God's inheritance. Paul borrows a phrase from the Old Testament to describe God's people. "You are a people holy to the Lord your God. The Lord has chosen you out of all the people on earth to be his people, *his treasured possession*." (Deuteronomy 7:6)

God brought his people out of Egypt and made them his covenant people. He didn't love them more than others. But he called them out so they could be a blessing to others. One on behalf of many. Now, Paul says, this reality is fulfilled in the church. We are called to be witnesses to God's mercy and grace!

If you are in Christ, you are God's treasured possession. He doesn't love you more than he loves others. But he wants you to wake up to your privilege and your call. God has placed an extraordinary value on you. We need to focus not only on what we *receive* from God but what we *mean* to God! Your value is not determined by your performance.

Faith says that you are someone of unlimited value—not because of what you do or how you look but because of what Christ has done. You matter—not because you have x number of friends or x number of likes but because Jesus is your friend. You're significant—not because you have outperformed other people but because you put your trust in the performance of Christ.

Edward Farrell went to Ireland to visit his uncle, who was about to celebrate his eightieth birthday. On the day of the birthday, Farrell and his uncle got up before dawn. They took a walk along the shores of Lake Killarney and stopped to watch the sunrise. They stood side by side, not saying a word. Staring straight at the rising sun. Suddenly, his uncle turned and went skipping down the road. He was radiant, beaming, smiling from ear to ear. Farrell said, "Uncle Seamus, you look really happy." "I am, lad." "Want to tell me why?" "Yes, you see, me Abba is very fond of me." Do you realize that your Abba is very fond of you?

Some days you may not feel like a treasured child of God. But this is your primary identity. You have to choose it every day. Many things threaten your sense of identity. Disappointment in yourself. Self-hatred. But you are not what others think. You're not even what you sometimes think about yourself. You are not what you do. You are not what you have. You have been known before you were conceived in your mother's womb. So don't let the pressure of social media cause you to feel down on yourself. Go back to the truth of who you really are.

The use of social media can be immensely helpful. But social media platforms also have the potential to counter the beautiful characteristics contained in the power of weakness. Let the user beware!

PRAYER:

"Father, help me to be in the world but not of the world. Help me not to conform to the ways of the world but to be transformed by the renewal of my mind through Christ. Keep me from using the gift of social media in ways that are sinful, selfish, and self-destructive. Teach me to spend more time with you and less time with social media. Father, I am so insecure when I look to myself or others for validation. I feel the tug of the world to assert who I am by promoting myself instead of promoting you. Teach me that my identity is safe only when I am defined by my relationship with you. Help me surrender once and for all my tendency to see my identity as something apart from you."

PRACTICAL SUGGESTIONS:

1. Fast from social media for one week.
2. Choose to limit your screen time to a certain number of hours each week.
3. Look for a specific way you can 'promote God' this week. Find someone to serve, someone to pray for, someone to share your faith with. Then get into action!

DISCUSSION QUESTIONS:

1. What are some positive impacts of social media? What are some negative impacts of social media?
   Contrasts between a biblical view of the power of weakness and the use of social media

BIBLICAL VIEW OF WEAKNESS	USE OF SOCIAL MEDIA
Promotes a spirit of humility	Moves us in the direction of pride
Urges caution about seeking spotlight	Moves us toward notoriety
Gives us a strong sense of identity	Confusion about identity

2. Read Ephesians 1:19. What does Paul mean by 'His glorious inheritance'?

3. What can we learn from the power of weakness about who we are? What are some practical ways we can resist the pressure of social media?

4. What impact does social media often have on our sense of identity?

CHAPTER 11

The Power of
Forgetting Yourself

***

**He who saves his life will lose it, but whoever loses his life will
find it.**

—Jesus

ONE OF THE DRIVING FORCES of our culture is the pressure to perform. We
want to know that we are somebody. That we count. That's why we assert ourselves. Advertise ourselves. We think, to get approval, we have to
achieve. We have to climb the ladder or else. We have to be skinny. We
have to be smart. We have to be successful. This drives us to perform.
We're looking for affirmation and attention. We want to show that we
measure up.

THE WORLD AS A MERITOCRACY

The world is based on the idea, "You are what you achieve. You are what
you accomplish. You are what you merit."

The world is a meritocracy. The world esteems the brightest and the
best. The world measures people's worth by how beautiful they are, how
much money they make, how many trophies they win. This can nudge us
to be obsessed with good grades or working out.

Our culture is constantly tugging at us, insisting that we need to
prove ourselves. But God says, "I want you to accept the performance-free

life once and for all. I want you to reject the meritocracy. I want you to be able to overcome the insecurity that comes with a life based on performance."

Satan will try to convince you that you need to prove yourself by working hard, obsessing over your grades, or posting a selfie with lots of filters. He'll try to persuade you that you can gain approval by marketing yourself to other people. But none of that really counts. What God thinks is the only thing that matters. His assessment is not based on you getting it all right but you trusting that Jesus got it all right.

OUR DANCING SHOES

Bryan Loritts points out that when we don't feel accepted for who we really are, we reach for our 'dancing shoes.' [22] To prove that we are 'somebody.' But there is a way to slay the beast of meritocracy. We learn to rest in God's love and approval. We don't have to live a life based on performance. We can choose a counterintuitive path. We can relax and just be who God made us to be. We don't have to prove ourselves.

AMY WINEHOUSE

Amy Winehouse was a once-in-a-generation talent.[23] For all her success, Amy was a miserable soul, battling alcoholism and drugs. She finally died of substance abuse. Performance didn't bring her fulfillment; in a weird sort of way, it only heightened her emptiness. But where did this emptiness come from? In a documentary on her life, Amy talks about the day her parents divorced and her dad walked out. She said that something in her died when her dad left. With no secure love from a father, Amy was left profoundly empty and vulnerable. Maybe you know her pain. You have no category for the words, "This is my child, whom I love; with her I am well pleased," because you've never heard them. Maybe your obsession with work, relationships, or good deeds is your attempt to find someone or something to say those words to you.

Depression and suicide are more and more common on college campuses in part because of the pressure to perform. Kathryn Dewitt was an Ivy League student at the University of Pennsylvania. She knew from kindergarten that she was expected to attend an elite college. From the New York Times: "(Once there) she awoke daily at 7:30 a.m. and often attended club meetings until as late as 10:00 p.m." She worked ten hours a week as part of her financial aid package, and studied furiously, especially for her multivariable calculus class.

Would she never measure up? Was she doing enough? Was she taking full advantage of all the opportunities? But then, she bombed her calculus midterm. The grade was so bad she was afraid she would fail the class. "I had a picture of my future, and as that future deteriorated, I stopped imagining another future." The pain of being less than what she thought she ought to be was unbearable. Depression twisted her logic, so she ended up taking her life.

This is a compelling reminder that a performance ethic won't take us where we want to go. Remember King Solomon? You talk about an overachiever. He built the Temple of God, one of the seven wonders of the ancient world. "I undertook great projects: I built houses for myself and planted vineyards. Yet when I surveyed all that my hands had done and what I had toiled to achieve, everything was meaningless, a chasing after the wind" (Ecclesiastes 2: 4–11). He couldn't find joy in what he had done. Because his life was predicated on performance. Let me urge you to run from a performance mindset. It's not about what you achieve—it's about who God has declared you to be. And he has declared you to be a person of infinite worth.

> N. T. Wright states, "We live in a world full of people struggling to be, or at least to appear strong, in order not to be weak; and we follow a gospel which says that when I am weak, then I am strong. And the gospel is the only thing that brings healing."

We not only embrace the performance mindset in relationship to the world. We sometimes embrace it in relation to God. We may feel driven to perform for God. We want to prove ourselves to God. So we work to perform our way into a right relationship with God. We know the world operates on the principle of performance, so we figure God does the same thing. We think we have to earn a relationship with God, just like we earn a grade in school. We think we have to perform for a relationship with God, just like we perform for a promotion at work.

We forget the gospel. We forget that we have a relationship with God not because of our performance but because of our faith in Jesus' performance.

Think about your spiritual report card. Chances are, there are some things you're not proud of. Maybe you had an abortion. Maybe you gossiped about someone else. Maybe you're stuck in a materialistic lifestyle. Maybe you're working to make sure you're pretty enough or handsome enough or smart enough. Your self-esteem is based on your performance. On being able to get it all right. But the good news of the gospel is that God is willing to embrace you, warts and all.

We have to dump the meritocracy. We have to ditch a life based on performance. Instead of looking to our performance, we need to look to Jesus' performance. Jesus performed everything that had to be done by dying on the cross and rising from the grave. Jesus can give you the performance-free life.

WHAT DID THE PHARI-SEE?

Jesus talks about two men. One man was a Pharisee, a man who prided himself on competing and comparing. He saw God as someone for whom he had to perform. He viewed himself as someone who had to outperform others in a spiritual contest. So he went up to the temple to pray. "God, I thank you that I am not like other people—robbers, evildoers, adulterers—or even like this tax collector. I fast twice a week and give a tenth of all I get." Notice the personal pronoun I.

The second man in Jesus' story is a tax collector. Tax collectors were the scum of Jewish society. They were social pariahs because they worked for the Roman government, extorting unjust taxes from their fellow Jews. The tax collector, says Jesus, stood at a distance. He wouldn't even look up to heaven. He beat his chest and said, "God, have mercy on me, a sinner." Now think about these two men. The Pharisee thinks performance is the way to a relationship with God. This means he has to announce his goodness. This means he has to compare himself to others. He can't get real with God or anybody else about his sin.

The tax collector is just the opposite. He knows he can't perform his way into a relationship with God. He knows he can only lean on God's grace. He knows that humility is the path to God. So here's what Jesus says about the two men. "I tell you that this man, rather than the other, went home justified before God. For all those who exalt themselves will be humbled, and those who humble themselves will be exalted." (Luke 18:14) Who went home justified? The man who understood his helplessness. The one who understood his poverty. The one who knew that performance is not the way to God. It isn't that he wasn't committed to honoring God—but he realized that his performance could never achieve righteousness.

There's freedom when you grasp the gospel. When you finally understand that the gospel is not good advice or good counsel or good teaching—the gospel is the good news that when you put your trust in Christ, you are saved. The only way to find yourself is to throw yourself on the mercy and grace of God.

The Potent Poison of Pride

According to the *National Geographic* website (their kids' version, that is), the pufferfish can inflate into a ball shape to evade predators. Also known as blowfish, these clumsy swimmers fill their elastic stomachs with huge amounts of water (and sometimes air) and blow themselves up to several times their normal size… But these blow-up fish aren't just cute. Most pufferfish contain a toxic substance that makes them foul-tasting and potentially deadly to other fish. The toxin is deadly to humans—1,200 times more deadly than cyanide. There is enough poison in one pufferfish to kill thirty adult humans, and there is no known antidote.

Like pufferfish, human beings can blow themselves up with pride and arrogance to make themselves look bigger than they are. And this pride can become toxic to a marriage, a church, or a friendship. No wonder the late Bible scholar John Stott once said, "Pride is your greatest enemy, humility is your greatest friend."

NOTHING TO PROVE

You don't have to prove yourself to other people. You don't have to prove yourself to God. God is the only qualifier there is. That doesn't mean you won't feel the pressure to perform. But God is the only one who can give you a fullness that can't be stripped away. If you are in Christ, you know you are a cherished child of the almighty God of the universe. You know that your identity and security are unimpeachable. You know that God is not in love with the future you. He's in love with the real you. He can love you and use you and transform you in ways you can't imagine. You know that God has liberated you from focusing on yourself.

We don't have to prove ourselves because Christ has already proven our value. It doesn't matter what any human court thinks. You're not defined by what your friends think. What your enemies think. What your critics think. The only thing that matters is God's verdict. That verdict was announced at the cross and in the resurrection. God announced that sin and death had been defeated. God announced that you don't have to perform, because Jesus has already performed everything that needed to be done.

We don't live *for* approval. We live *from* approval. If we're perfectly accepted as we are, you may wonder why we would feel any need or motivation to change. Many of us were taught that God would love us if we changed. But the reality is that God loves us with no strings attached, and then offers the power to transform. The engine of change is God's love. The goal of change is not God's love. God's love is the gift that makes the change possible.

NO MORE QUALIFYING

This means that we're done with qualifying. We don't have to qualify ourselves because God qualified us through Jesus. The love of Christ reminds us that our qualification is in Christ. "We are confident of all this because of our great trust in God through Christ. It is not that we think we are qualified to do anything on our own. Our qualification comes from God." (2 Corinthians 3:4–5)

But how is it that God qualifies us? The explanation is found in Corinthians: "For God made Christ, who never sinned, to be the offering for our sin, so that we could be made right with God through Christ." (2 Corinthians 5:21) God made him who had no sin to be sin for us so that in him we might become the righteousness of God. What does God see when he looks at us? God knew that we were sinners. God didn't ignore our sin. But he judged it by pouring out his wrath on his Son. And here's what happened at the cross. It's called the great exchange. Jesus took on our sin in exchange for his righteousness.

Our daughter, Haley, graduated from college a few years ago. She received a scholarship that gave her a full ride to college. Every semester, we got a statement that itemized all her expenses. At the bottom, the costs were tallied. In the 'You Owe' box it always said zero. I loved that zero. This is one part of the great exchange. Jesus paid the price for our sin so that when we look in the 'You Owe' box it reads zero. But that's only part of the great exchange. It's not enough to have a zero in the sin box. Clearing our debt was half the job. We needed more than just removing our guilt. We needed perfection we didn't possess. This is where Jesus stepped in. He not only died to forgive us. He lived a perfect life so that his perfection could be credited to us.

Christ took our punishment and gave us his righteousness. So what does God see? In the Christian, he sees thirty-three years of Christ's perfect life dripping off of us. Christ lived a perfect life and died a perfect death so that his perfect record could be credited to imperfect sinners. This perfect record is what God sees when he looks at us. Christ is our qualification.

God took an eternity of what we deserved and unleashed it on his Son so he could give us an eternity of what we don't deserve. God looked on Jesus as though he had lived my life so he could look on me as if I had lived Jesus' life. Through Jesus, God sees me just as if I had never sinned, just as if I had always obeyed. The death of Jesus paid for our sins, paid our debt. But that's not all. The life of Jesus, the obedience of Jesus, was deposited into our account. So that we're unbelievably wealthy.

You can get past a life of qualifying and comparing. But it starts by embracing the love of Christ. His love for you has nothing to do with your performance. Of course, he wants you to follow him and obey him and serve him. But those aren't things you do to gain his love. They are things you do in response to his singular, performance-free love.

You can shake loose from the posturing and the perfectionism. You can be free from qualifying and comparing. So ditch your try-harder tactics and rest in God's love. Jesus is inviting you to stop performing for him and start abiding in him.

The only way to find ourselves is to lose ourselves. Listen again to C.S. Lewis.

There are no real personalities apart from God. Until you have given up yourself to Him you will not have a real self. Sameness is to be found most among the most 'natural' men, not among those who surrender to Christ. How monotonously alike all the great tyrants and conquerors have been; how gloriously different are the saints. But there must be a real giving up of the self. You must throw it away 'blindly' so to speak. Christ will indeed give you a real personality; but you must not go to Him for the sake of that. As long as your own personality is what you are bothering about you are not going to Him at all. The very first step is to try to forget about the self altogether.[24]

PRAYER:

"Father, give me a healthy view of myself. Help me not to think too much of myself or too little of myself, but instead, not to think much about myself at all. Teach me the paradox that when I lose myself for Your sake, I find myself. Show me the path to forgetting myself."

PRACTICAL SUGGESTION:

1. Memorize these scriptures that remind us of a healthy view of ourselves:

   1 Corinthians 4:7: "What do you have that you did not receive?"

   Romans 12:3: "For by the grace given me I say to every one of you: Do not think of yourself more highly than you ought, but rather think of yourself with sober judgment, in accordance with the faith God has distributed to each of you."

DISCUSSION QUESTIONS:

1. What is your greatest challenge in learning to forget yourself?
2. Read Luke 11:13. How can the Holy Spirit assist you in learning to deny yourself?
3. Have you known someone who seemed to genuinely forget about himself or herself? What was that person like?
4. What can you do today to exercise the principle of forgetting yourself?

CHAPTER 12

The Power of Foolishness

✳✳✳

The foolishness of God is wiser than man's wisdom. The weakness of God is stronger than man's strength.

—The apostle Paul

THE TRUTH IS, I CAN find the weakness of Jesus to be off-putting, or at least something I'm not always comfortable with.

MY COMPLAINT AGAINST JESUS THE PUSHOVER

Jesus seems like a pushover most of his life. He just keeps working out of a position of weakness. He retreats when he needs to advance. He turns the other cheek. He doesn't know the first thing about how to get things done. He's far too passive. Too quick to let others have their way.

The whole thing is really hard for me to stomach. What's wrong with him, anyway? He needs a course in assertiveness training. He refuses to turn stones to bread. He could turn his enemies to mince-meat, but he won't do it. He spends most of his time with weaklings. People who are rejected. Doesn't he know you need to be more aggressive, to work harder to get things done your way? He just seems so foolish.

But of course, most of all, there's this cross business. Of all the stupid decisions I've ever heard of, why would he let himself die on a cross? I just don't understand him. He had every opportunity to prove himself to be a king, and then this. Of all the boneheaded things he could have done, this takes the cake! Why not just go ahead and rout the Romans? Why not go ahead and zap the Pharisees? He must have gotten some bad advice somewhere along the way.

Well, the good thing is, I've learned better. None of this foolishness for me! I've learned to play it smart, not dumb like he did. I know how to push harder than he did. I know how to operate from a position of strength instead of weakness. Thank goodness I know how to avoid the pitfalls that left him so vulnerable.

But the most frustrating thing is that his followers never seemed to wise up. They climbed onto this weakness bandwagon. They had this crazy idea that power comes from weakness, too. Not one of the New Testament books recommends power lunches. Or power suits. Or power moves. I don't like him, this God of weakness.

I still don't much care for the Jesus story. I don't like to think about Mary being accused of having an illegitimate child: it makes me feel like I should reach out to women with crisis pregnancies. I don't like to think about Jesus being born in a barn: it makes me feel like I should reach out to the poor. I don't like to think about Jesus spending his time with the weak: it makes me feel like I should spend my time with the wounded.

I don't like to think about Jesus not pushing his agenda: it makes me think I need to give in more often. I don't like to think about Jesus dying on a messy cross: it makes me think I might actually have to take one up myself.

It's all pretty insane, after all, don't you think? It's all a bunch of nonsense, this idea of strength through weakness. Everybody knows the only way to get along in this world is to strut your stuff.

I can't wait to get past the Jesus story so I can get past this weakness thing. I can forget that Jesus was born in weakness and return to a posture of strength. I can go back to flexing my muscles. Trying to build my net worth. Working to have things my way. Making sure I always have respectability. Building a network of friends with power. I can just dismiss the foolishness of God.

But I am the one who is foolish. God honors the weak. God works to protect the weak. Jesus died in weakness. Jesus spent time with the weak. And his followers care for those who are weak.

AN EXERCISE IN SELF-DEMOTION

It's easy to spend our lives in self-promotion, when a better strategy is to choose the path of demotion. And I'm convinced one of the best ways to embrace this strategy is to spend time with the weak.

God has always been a champion of the underdog. Psalm 12:5 says, "Because of the oppression of the weak and the groaning of the needy, I will now arise, says the LORD. I will protect them from those who malign them." Psalm 72:13 says, "He will take pity on the weak and the needy and save the needy from death."

Now those are not isolated examples. In fact, I went through the entire New Testament. I discovered the theme of weakness all the way from Matthew to Revelation. It's in every single book. Let me show you. Let's start with Matthew.

THE ROLL CALL OF WEAKNESS IN THE NEW TESTAMENT

Matthew tells us about Jesus calling up a little child and having the child stand in the middle of the people. And then Jesus says, "...whoever humbles himself like this child is the greatest in the kingdom of heaven. And whoever welcomes a little child like this in my name welcomes me." (Matthew 18:4–5) Jesus says you need to welcome the weak. Because when you welcome the weak, you're welcoming me.

What about the Gospel according to Mark? Mark writes to the Romans, who hated weakness. But over and over in Mark's gospel, Jesus says things like, 'Whoever wants to become great among you must be your servant." (Mark 10:43)

In Luke, it's the little people who are honored. Stinky old shepherds are the first to hear the news of baby Jesus. Everything gets turned upside down. The rich and famous trade places with the not so rich and famous. The heroes of Luke's gospel are the poor and the women and the outsiders and the sinners.

In John, it's the broken people Jesus speaks to. Like the woman who's been through five divorces in John 4. Or the woman caught in the act of adultery in John 8.

Look at the church in the Book of Acts. It's a church that celebrates weakness. Nobody claims his possessions are his own: they share everything they have.

Then there's Romans. Paul says he is not ashamed of the gospel of Christ, even though the symbol of the gospel is a man crucified on a cross.

The theme of weakness just keeps rolling in the New Testament. In Galatians, Paul is crucified with Christ. (Galatians 2:20)

In Ephesians, he's the very least of all the saints.

In Philippians, Paul's goal is to share in Christ's sufferings, becoming like him in his death. (Philippians 3:20)

In Colossians, Paul says he welcomes the chance to share in Christ's sufferings. (Colossians 1:24) I wonder how that would play in the church today? What if the elders got up every week and said, "You need to welcome the chance to share in Christ's sufferings." What would we think? We run from suffering; we would never think of running toward it.

In 1 and 2 Thessalonians, weak Christians are powerful in the middle of suffering.

In 1 and 2 Timothy, Paul says, *Listen, rich people: don't be arrogant or put your hope in wealth.* (1 Timothy 6:17)

In Titus, Paul is a slave of God.

In Philemon, Paul urges Philemon to treat Onesimus not as a slave but as a brother.

Hebrews is jam-packed with weakness. Jesus is the high priest who is able to sympathize with our weaknesses. Jesus dies in weakness, enduring the cross.

In James, God says that true religion is to care for the orphans and widows in their weakness. (James 1:22)

In 1 and 2 Peter, Christians are told to follow in the steps of the one who was abused and wounded.

In 1 John, we're told to lay down our lives for our brothers. (1 John 3:16)

In Jude, Jesus is the one who keeps us from falling. (Jude verse 24)

Revelation is written to people so weak they're being slaughtered for their faith.

Now I hope you realize that this is not just a list. Weakness is mentioned in every single book of the New Testament. And here's why: Weakness is close to the heart of God.

RECEIVING THE BLESSING OF HELPING THE WEAK

A pediatrician in Germany trained young people to work with mentally handicapped children. At the end of the one-year training period, he asked them to fill out a survey. He said, "What changes have taken place in your life since you became totally involved with disabled people?" Here are some of their answers:

"For the first time in my life, I feel I am doing something really significant."

"I'm more responsive now to human suffering and it arouses in me the desire to help."

"It's made me question what's really important in life."

"In serving the disabled, I've discovered myself."

"My own little problems don't seem so important anymore, and I've learned to accept myself with all my inadequacies. Especially I thank God that he has shown me that love can achieve more than hate or force."

We usually think about what ministry does for other people. But some-times, we forget what serving other people does for us. Maybe this is what Paul had in mind when he said this: "In everything I did, I showed you that by this kind of hard work we must help the weak, remember the words the Lord Jesus himself said: 'It is more blessed to give than to receive.'" (Acts 20:35) The paradox is that when we care for the weak, we often receive more than they do.

GIVING THE BLESSING OF HELPING THE WEAK

We need to give the blessing of spending time with the weak. "And we urge you, brothers, warn those who are idle, encourage the timid, help the weak..." (1 Thessalonians 5:14) We not only receive a blessing when we care for the weak—we provide a blessing. Whenever we care for the weak, we are doing the work of God. God has always cared for the weak. His heart has always been for the weak.

"Defend the cause of the weak and fatherless; maintain the rights of the oppressed. Rescue the weak and needy; deliver them from the hand of the wicked." (Psalm 82:3–4) Do you realize when you reach out to the weak, you are sharing in the heart of God? When you take a meal to a person in need, you're emulating God. When you visit a shut-in, you're personifying the spirit of God.

God has always wanted his people to look after the needs of the weak. Ezekiel challenged the shepherds of Israel. He challenged their neglect of the weak. He said, "You have not strengthened the weak or healed the sick or bound up the injured. You have not brought back the strays or searched for the lost." (Ezekiel 34:4)

God calls us to help the weak because that's what he's always done. Jesus touched the lepers nobody else would touch. He had dinner with sinners nobody else would eat with. He let a sinful woman wash his feet when nobody else wanted her in the house.

My wife, Holly, is one of my heroes. Through the years, Holly has tirelessly looked after our special needs daughter, Hannah. This included (and often still includes) doing everything for Hannah that she could not do herself—bathing her, dressing her, fixing her hair, getting her to school, often having to feed Hannah when she needed help, seeing Hannah to the bathroom repeatedly during the day, changing Hannah's dirty diapers (even into Hannah's adulthood), and lovingly caring for all of Hannah's needs.

My friends, Michelle Branum and Tina Silvaggio, discovered a need in downtown Dallas associated with the Salvation Army. Dozens of women were transitioning from the state prison to a halfway house before later being released into public life. Many of the women were repeat offenders, with criminal records for drugs, theft, or prostitution. Most came from extremely dysfunctional homes.

Following the lead of Jo Wicks, who had founded the ministry and come to be known to the women as 'Mama Jo,' Michelle and Tina carried out a ministry of service to these women coming out of prison. They brought games and small gifts. They arranged monthly devotionals with the women. They introduced them to Christ. They ministered to some of the weakest women in the world.

Our daughter, Haley, is a medical missionary in Mexico. She serves as a nurse in a tiny twenty-five-bed hospital in the Sierra Madre mountains. The hospital serves the needs of the Tarahumara Indians, who live in destitute conditions. The Tarahumara people suffer from an infant mortality rate of 50 percent.

On one occasion, a couple brought their twin daughters into the hospital, seeking help. One of the girls was reasonably healthy, the other was severely malnourished. The parents had been forced to make a decision: which one of their children would live and which one would die because they didn't have enough food to sustain both. Thanks to the work of the hospital, both girls were nourished and brought to health.

The Tarahuma Mission Hospital was established by Dr. Mike Berkeley in 2002. 'Dr. Mike' had served as the United States ski team physician in

Aspen, Colorado. Renowned for his skill in repairing broken legs and joints, he performed procedures on world-class athletes. But he wasn't content to do this. I listened to him describe his calling from God and his vision for the hospital. He said, "I didn't want my tombstone to read, 'He fixed a lot of knees.'" Dr. Mike received the gift of serving the weak. He literally went from serving some of the most powerful people in the world to serving some of the weakest in the world.

The reality is, if we were to ask God to put us to work, he would begin pointing out places right and left for us to spring into action. Those places are everywhere. Denying ourselves isn't an occasional option; it's a way of life. This is the death we must die. It's daily dying. So we can find life.

Nik Wallenda got huge TV ratings a few years ago. He walked across Niagara Falls on a high wire. The next year, he became the first man to walk a wire across the Grand Canyon. He's a strong Christian. But how do you humble yourself when you're the best in the world at something and millions tune in to cheer your every step? Huge crowds come to these events, and they leave huge loads of garbage in their wake.

After his walk, Wallenda didn't head for a limousine. He spent hours walking around, picking up the trash his fans had strewn. This was what he said.

> Three hours of cleaning up debris is good for my soul. Humility does not come naturally to me. So if I have to force myself into situations that are humbling, so be it... I do it... because it's a way to keep from tripping. As a follower of Jesus, I see Him washing the feet of others. I do it because if I don't serve others I'll be serving nothing but my ego. [25]

Of course, serving others often involves huge challenges. Kevin Miller is a pastor who posted this question to his friends on Facebook: "What makes it hard for you to serve other people?" They gave great answers:

"Serving is hard when it doesn't fit into my schedule or plan. Like when I want to go for a walk or take a long bath, but my aging parent needs me to sort their meds, run an errand, or simply be with them." "It's hard when their need seems endless. I don't want to risk helping/serving because I may get sucked in. Being swallowed up in the serving and not getting to be the me I think I am or should be." "There is such limited energy left after a demanding workday meeting our basic responsibilities (whether with young kids or in the corporate world). How do you balance the need for rest and self-care with serving others?"

But Miller's favorite answer was this one: "Others." When others can make it seem impossible to serve them, I remember that Christ washed the feet of Judas, who would betray him, and Peter, who would deny him. Can I do less for those who are undesirable or even hostile?

Who are the greatest people? The mother who changes the dirty diaper of her child with love. The friend who changes the bedpan of the hurting patient. The teacher who wipes the snotty nose of a little child. The Christian who takes time to befriend and teach someone who is lost.

I mentioned Oliver de Vinck earlier. Oliver was a helpless invalid for thirty-eight years before he died. There were a lot of people who would say that Oliver was just a drain on the resources of the world. A drain on his family. A drain on society. A needless parasite sucking dry the resources of people and organizations around him. But it's strange: Oliver's family didn't feel that way. They felt Oliver was the greatest teacher they ever had. That they learned lessons in compassion from Oliver.

In fact, his mother wrote:

Oliver was always a hopeless case, yet he was such a precious gift for our whole family. God has chosen the foolish things of the world to confound the wise, and God has chosen the weak things of the world to confound the things which are mighty. This child had no apparent usefulness or meaning, and the world would reject him as being an unproductive burden. But he was a holy innocent, a child of Light. Looking at him, I saw the power of powerlessness. His total helplessness speaks to our deepest hearts, calls us not merely to pious emotions but to service. Through this child, I felt bound to Christ crucified—yes, and also to all those who suffer in the world...

This is the message for those who choose to honor the weak!

THE BALLOON STOMP

Robert Roberts tells about a fourth-grade class where the teacher introduced a game called the balloon stomp. A balloon was tied to each child's leg. The object of the game was for the students to try to pop everybody else's balloons while protecting their own. The last child with an intact balloon would be the winner. A class of ten-year-olds came in, and the game was over in a few seconds. Only one balloon was still inflated.

Then a class of developmentally challenged children was brought in. They were each given a balloon and the same instructions. But this game went much differently. Instead of fighting each other off, the kids got the idea that they were supposed to help one another pop balloons. So they formed a balloon stomp co-op. The kids helped each other stomp each other's balloons. And when the last balloon was popped, everybody cheered. They had developed a brilliant alternative scoring system. In the new system, students didn't score points **against** each other but **with** each other. Instead of seeing each other as opponents, they saw each other as teammates. So, who got the game right, and who got the game wrong? What's the best way to keep score?

Some people groups are intent on getting it right. I love the example of the children of the Aborigines in Australia. They engage in footraces. But they so dislike 'disgracing' each other that the faster runners deliberately slow down to encourage the slower ones. In Brazil, the Xavante people have a ritual involving two sets of people carrying heavy logs. To us, it would look like a race. But if one group falls behind, the other will wait for them so they can complete the run together.

Holly and I took our handicapped daughter to camp for the first time. We waited to register Hannah. Everybody on the deck of the cabin was weak. Kids with cerebral palsy. Kids who couldn't talk. Kids who couldn't change their own diapers. Kids with Down syndrome. Kids with hearing aids and very limited IQs. Kids the world would label as weak.

But there was power on that deck like I've never seen in my life. There was no pretense in any of those kids. They didn't care what they were wearing. They didn't care what they looked like. They were smiling and having a good time. They would go up and hug each other, even though they'd never met before. A little girl with Down's syndrome took my hand and led me over to one of the counselors and put the counselor's hand in mine. Nobody worried about making any impressions. There wasn't an ounce of self-consciousness. But there was love. There was affection. There was joy. Some people would describe it as a collection of weak people. But I would describe it as the strongest group of kids I've ever been around.

"God chose the foolish things of the world to shame the wise. He chose the weak things of the world to shame the strong." (1 Corinthians 1:27)

PRAYER:

"Father, give me a heart for the weak. Show me what you want me to learn from them. Help me never to condescend to them, but instead, to receive from them what you want to give me. Show me the power of the powerless."

PRACTICAL SUGGESTIONS:

1. Using a concordance, look up all the references to 'weak' and 'weakness' that you can find in the Bible.

2. Ask God to give you a heart for the weak and powerless, and to show you ways in which you can serve the weak and powerless.

DISCUSSION QUESTIONS:

1. What is your most important takeaway from reading this book?
2. What life change do you plan to make as a result of this study?
3. How can you honor the weak going forward?

Appendix 1

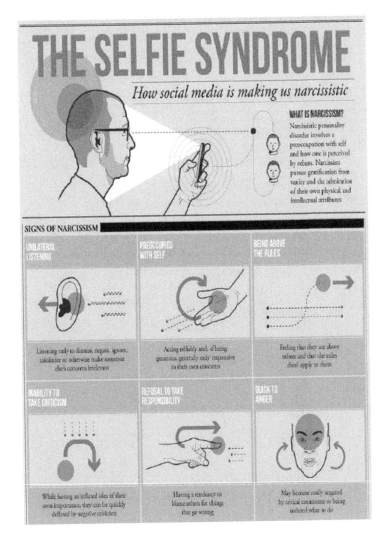

Appendix 2

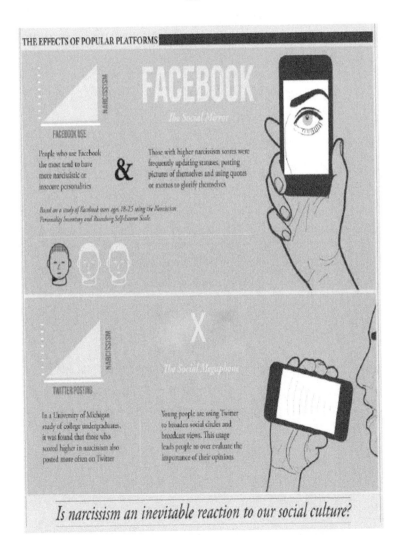

THE EFFECTS OF POPULAR PLATFORMS

FACEBOOK

The Social Mirror

NARCISSISM

FACEBOOK USE

People who use Facebook the most tend to have more narcissistic or insecure personalities

&

Those with higher narcissism scores were frequently updating statuses, posting pictures of themselves and using quotes or mottos to glorify themselves

Based on a study of Facebook users ages 18-25 using the Narcissism Personality Inventory and Rosenberg Self-Esteem Scale.

X

The Social Megaphone

NARCISSISM

TWITTER POSTING

In a University of Michigan study of college undergraduates, it was found that those who scored higher in narcissism also posted more often on Twitter

Young people are using Twitter to broaden social circles and broadcast views. This usage leads people to over-evaluate the importance of their opinions

Is narcissism an inevitable reaction to our social culture?

Acknowledgments

I'm indebted to my wife Holly, whose servant heart is a demonstration of Jesus' upside down principle of life. She lives out before me and others the choice to move downward, rather than upward.

Endnotes

1. Christopher Devink, *The Power of the Powerless* (Crossroad, 2002).

2. Henri Nouwen, *Adam* (Orbis Books, 2012).

3. Christine Hall, "Rice Students Build Replica of Peter Parker's Bedroom," *TMC News* (2018).

4. C.S. Lewis, *Mere Christianity* (1942).

5. Garrett Fagan, *The History of Ancient Rome* (The Teaching Company, 1999).

6. Dave Harvey, *Rescuing Ambition* (Crossway, 2010).

7. Tom Farrey, *Game On: The All-American Race to Make Champions of Our Children* (ESPN, 2008).

8. Joni Eareckson Tada, "Joy Hard Won," *Decision* (March 2000).

9. Chuck Colson, "God Used My Greatest Defeat," sermon illustration, taken from the sermon "The Gravy Train Gospel," *Preaching Today* (accessed December 2014).

10. Francisco Roballo, "Blue Eyes and Brown Eyes: The Jane Elliott Experiment," *Exploring the Mind* (December 2022).

11. John Ortberg, *The Me I Want to Be* (Zondervan, 2009).

12. Jennifer Kennedy Dean, "The Power of a Crucified Life," *Charisma* (July 2014).

13. Timothy Keller, *The Freedom of Self-Forgetfulness* (10 Publishing, 2012).

14. C.S. Lewis, *Mere Christianity* (1942).

15. Hugh Jackman, Adapted from Stephen Galloway, "Hugh Jackman on His Surprising Hollywood BFFs and Mother's Abandonment," *The Hollywood Reporter*.

16. Jean Twenge and Keith Campbell, *The Narcissism Epidemic* (Free Press, 2009).

17. John Starke, *The Secret Place of Thunder* (Zondervan, 2023).

18. Marguerite Ward, "This Princeton Professor Posted His CV Of Failures For The World To See," CNBC.com. *(4-27-16)*

19. Mark Sayers, *The Vertical Self* (Thomas Nelson, 2010).

20. "Why Instagram Is the Worst Social Media for Mental Health," *Time* (May 2017).

21. Alan Noble, *You Are Not Your Own* (Intervarsity, 2021).

22. Bryan Loritts, *Saving the Saved* (Zondervan, 2016).

23. Desiree Ibekwe, "Looking Again at Amy Winehouse, Ten Years After Her Death," *New York Times* (December 2021).

24. C.S. Lewis, *Mere Christianity* (1942).

25. Nik Wallenda with David Ritz, *Balance: A Story of Faith, Family, and Life on the Line* (New York: FaithWords, 2013), 207–8.

Made in the USA
Middletown, DE
07 March 2024

50417809R00086